KYFFIN

DAN SYLW · IN VIEW

Darlithoedd DATHLU Canmlwyddiant Syr Kyffin Williams RA
Lectures to CELEBRATE the Centenary of Sir Kyffin Williams RA

Gomer

First published in 2018 by GOMER,
Llandysul, Ceredigion SA44 4JL

ISBN 978 1 78562 266 3

A CIP record for this title is available from the British Library.

This book is published with the financial support of the
Welsh Books Council.

Printed and bound in Wales at
Gomer Press, Llandysul, Ceredigion
www.gomer.co.uk

Cynnwys / Contents

Rhagair

Wedi marwolaeth Syr Kyffin Williams yn 2006 a ffurfio Ymddiriedolaeth yn ei enw yn 2007, sefydlwyd Darlith Goffa Syr Kyffin, darlith i'w chynnal yn flynyddol, i'w anrhydeddu ac i gofio am ei gyfraniad aruthrol i fyd celf Cymru fel arlunydd, cymwynaswr, awdur a darlithydd.

Eleni, wrth i Gymru ddathlu canmlwyddiant geni Syr Kyffin (1918-2018), John Kyffin Williams neu Kyffin fel yr hoffai gael ei alw, mae'n llawenydd i'r Ymddiriedolaeth fod Gomer, wedi ymgymeryd â chyhoeddi y llyfr hwn o ddarlithoedd a draddodwyd rhwng 2007 a 2018, darlithoedd sy'n ymdrin â gwahanol agweddau o fywyd a gwaith "Kyffin o Fôn", cawr byd celfyddyd Cymru, gydag un o'r darlithoedd yn ymwneud â dylanwad gwaith celf ar farddoniaeth cyfaill mawr Kyffin, y bardd R. S. Thomas. Ymhyfrydai Kyffin yn wastadol yn safon cyhoeddiadau celf Gomer ac mae'r cyhoeddiad hwn yn dilyn yn eu traddodiad gorau — cyhoeddiad swyddogol Ymddiriedolaeth Syr Kyffin ym mlwyddyn ei ganmlwyddiant. Traddodwyd y darlithoedd yn Oriel Kyffin Williams yn Oriel Môn yn Llangefni.

Ar ran yr Ymddiriedolaeth, rwy'n estyn diolch twymgalon i'r darlithwyr oll.

Ni welodd Cymru arlunydd mor gynhyrchiol ac mor fasnachol lwyddiannus â John Kyffin Williams ac mae hi mor briodol eleni fod Cymru, wrth ddathlu ei ganmlwyddiant, yn cofio ac yn diolch am waith athrylith. Bu'n arlunio yng ngwledydd Prydain, gan gofnodi pobl, tirlun, arfordiroedd a byd natur Cymru a Phatagonia yn arbennig, yn ogystal â mannau eraill yn y byd megis yr Eidal a Ffrainc, Groeg ac Awstria, a gwneud hynny yn ddi-ball am drigain mlynedd, gan fynnu fod cariad at ei bwnc yn hanfodol i bob gwir arlunydd.

Gosodwyd Darlith Flynyddol Kyffin ar seiliau cadarn o'r dechrau gan yr Athro Derec Llwyd Morgan a fu'n Gadeirydd yr Ymddiriedolaeth ers ei sefydlu yn 2007 hyd 2016. Mawr yw ein dyled iddo am ei weledigaeth a'i ddygnwch ac iddo ef a'i gydymddiriedolwyr am sicrhau fod y ddarlith flynyddol yn dilyn patrwm o gael ei thraddodi yn Gymraeg ac yn Saesneg bob yn ail flwyddyn.

Dros y blynyddoedd cafwyd darlithoedd cofiadwy a threiddgar gyda thraethu coeth gan ddarlithwyr penigamp, fel y tystia eu henwau ar y dudalen gynnwys, pob darlithydd yn ei dro ac yn ei thro yn ymdrin â gwahanol agweddau ar gelfyddyd Syr Kyffin a byd celf yn gyffredinol.

Wele yma ddarlithoedd sy'n gyfraniad pwysig er ymestyn ein dealltwriaeth o gamp a dawn Kyffin, y gŵr a gyhoeddodd ei fod yn peintio yn Gymraeg! — Kyffin ein trysor cenedlaethol.

Dyma gyfrol i'w thrysori.

David Meredith
Cadeirydd Ymddiriedolaeth Syr Kyffin Williams
Mai 2018

Foreword

Following the death of Sir Kyffin Williams in 2006 and the formation of the Sir Kyffin Williams Trust in 2007, the new trust established the Sir Kyffin Williams Memorial Lecture as an annual event, to honour his name and to mark his unique contribution to the arts in Wales as an artist, benefactor, author and lecturer.

This year, as Wales celebrates the centenary of Sir John Kyffin Williams, RA (1918-2018), or Kyffin as he preferred to be called, the members of the Sir Kyffin Williams Trust rejoice in the knowledge that Gomer Press of Llandysul and Carmarthen have prepared this book of nine lectures given at Oriel Kyffin Williams in Oriel Môn, Llangefni, between 2009 and 2018. The lectures, five of which are in English and four in Welsh, deal with different aspects of Sir Kyffin's life and work, including the influence of art on the poetry of Kyffin's close friend, the poet R.S. Thomas. Sir Kyffin often commented on the high standard of design and production of the Gomer Press books on art, and the publication of these lectures follows in that noble tradition. This book is the official publication of the Sir Kyffin Williams Trust in this centenary year.

John Kyffin Williams was one of the most successful and productive artists that Wales has ever produced, and it is very fitting that Wales celebrates his centenary and remembers his contributions to art. He painted throughout the British Isles and recorded the people, the landscape, and the seascape of Wales and Patagonia, as well as drawing and painting in countries such as Italy, France, Greece and Austria. He painted relentlessly for over sixty years, always maintaining that an artist had to love his subject matter: 'If you love something, you can communicate – that's love; people who don't love anything cannot communicate.'

The Kyffin Williams Memorial Lecture was firmly established from the outset by the founding Trust chairman, Professor Derec Llwyd Morgan, who served as chairman between 2007 and 2016. We are in his debt for his inspired leadership, and to him and his fellow Trust members for setting the pattern of alternating Welsh and English lectures.

Over the years, memorable and inspired lectures have been delivered by speakers of note, as can be seen from the names on the contents page, each lecturer in turn dealing with different aspects of Kyffin's work. On behalf of the Trust, I thank them all for their contribution and I am honoured to be listed among them.

You will find in the following pages lectures that are an important contribution to our understanding of the genius of Kyffin Williams, our national treasure – Kyffin, who told us, 'I paint in Welsh.'

This is a volume to be cherished.

David Meredith
Chairman of the Sir Kyffin Williams Trust
May 2018

Diolchiadau

Dymuna Ymddiriedolaeth Syr Kyffin Williams ddiolch o galon i Mrs. Diana Dunstan am y rhodd o bortread o Syr Kyffin Williams gan ei ddiweddar ŵr Bernard Dunstan RA.

Diolchwn i Gomer am gyhoeddi'r gyfrol i ddathlu canmlwyddiant Syr Kyffin, yn arbennig i Meirion Davies a'r Dr Ashley Owen o'r wasg am eu cymorth golygyddol.

Diolchwn hefyd i Ann a John Smith ac i Cathrin Williams am eu cymorth ymarferol.

Diolch yn arbennig i awduron y darlithoedd am eu cymorth parod.

Thanks

The Sir Kyffin Williams Trust wishes to thank Mrs. Diana Dunstan, for the gift of a portrait of Sir Kyffin by her late husband Bernard Dunstan RA.

We thank Gomer for publishing this volume in the centenary year of Sir Kyffin's birth, with special thanks to Meirion Davies and Dr Ashley Owen for their editorial assistance.

We would also like to thank Ann and John Smith and Cathrin Williams for their practical assistance.

Finally, we are very grateful to the authors of each lecture for their ready co-operation.

Sir John Kyffin Williams
(1918 – 2006)

Ganwyd Kyffin Williams yn Tanygraig, Llangefni, Ynys Môn, ar 9 Mai 1918, yn ail fab i Henry Inglis Wynne Williams (1870-1942), rheolwr banc, a'i wraig Essyllt Mary (1883-1964), merch Richard Hughes Williams, rheithor Llansadwrn. Ganwyd eu mab cyntaf Owen Richard Inglis Williams (Dick) ym 1916 a bu farw 1982. Ymfalchïai Kyffin Williams yn ei wreiddiau teuluol dwfn yn naear Cymru, ym Môn (teulu ei dad), ym Maldwyn (o ble y deuai'r enw Kyffin) ac yn ardal Ystrad Fflur yng Ngheredigion (lle claddwyd ei hen hen nain ar ochr ei fam). Perthynai ar ddwy ochr ei deulu i nifer helaeth o ficeriaid a rheithoriaid eglwysig a mawrygai eu gwasanaeth i'w cyd-ddyn. Roedd unigolion lliwgar hefyd ymhlith ei hynafiaid, megis Thomas Williams (1737-1802), y gŵr a ddatblygodd ddiwydiant copr Mynydd Parys ym Môn.

Wedi cyfnod byr yn 1924 yn Ysgol Moreton Hall ger y Waun, lle roedd ei dad yn rheolwr banc, mynychodd Kyffin ysgol gynradd ym Mae Trearddur, Môn (1925-1931). Rhwng 1931 a 1936 bu'n ddisgybl preswyl yn Ysgol yr Amwythig. Wedi gadael yr ysgol, lle bu'n anhapus oherwydd teimladau o unigrwydd ac athrawon gor-awdurdodol, trefnodd ei dad iddo ymuno ag asiantaeth tir 'Yale and Hardcastle' ym Mhwllheli (1937-1939), cyfnod a'i galluogodd i ddod i adnabod cefn gwlad Llŷn o'i gartref, erbyn hynny yn Abererch. Ar anogaeth ei fam ymunodd â'r Capten Jack Jones a Helfa'r Ynysfor yn ardal Aberglaslyn, a bu'n cerdded y mynyddoedd yn benrhydd ym mhob tywydd, yn hela llwynogod a dod i adnabod pob cilfach a phant, profiad amheuthun i arlunydd tirluniau. Dywedid am Kyffin Williams pan oedd yn peintio mynydd, y gwyddai beth oedd yr ochr arall i'r llechwedd a'i hwynebai - gwelai'r darlun yn llawn.

Ym 1937 comisiynwyd ef fel Ail Lifftenant y Ffiwsilwyr Cymreig (TA), ond cafodd ei ollwng o'r fyddin yn 1940 oherwydd iddo gael trawiad epileptig. Bu'n dioddef yn ddewr o'r aflwydd epilepsi gydol ei oes. Yn y cyfnod hwn cafodd gyfeillgarwch triw Sandy Livingstone-Learmouth o Dremadog. Sandy anogodd Kyffin i ymuno â'r fyddin diriogaethol. Bu'r ddau, er mawr ddifyrrwch iddynt, yn llunio limrigau 'Crawshaw-Bailey', penillion digri i'w canu ar y dôn Mochyn Du. Cyhoeddwyd y casgliad yn y llyfr *Boyo Ballads* (Gwasg Excellent/Llyfrgell Genedlaethol Cymru, 1995). Gwelir gwaith cartŵn ardderchog Kyffin Williams yn y llyfr hwn.

Wrth gael ei ollwng o'r fyddin y cyngor a gafodd Kyffin gan y doctor milwrol oedd: 'Williams, gan eich bod mewn gwirionedd yn abnormal credaf y byddai'n syniad da i chi droi at arlunio', geiriau y câi Kyffin, pan yn benblaenor y celfyddydau yng Nghymru, fwynhad mawr o'u hailadrodd. Yn hydref 1941 aeth Kyffin yn fyfyriwr i Ysgol Gelf y Slade, oedd wedi symud o Lundain i Amgueddfa'r Ashmolean yn Rhydychen oherwydd y rhyfel. Yn yr Ashmolean, wrth syllu'n ddwys ar lun o'r 'Atgyfodiad' gan Piero della Francesca, cymaint oedd yr effaith emosiynol ar Kyffin fel yr wylodd yn hidl. Fel y dywedodd, dyma oedd ei 'ffordd i Ddamascus'. Sylweddolodd am y tro cyntaf nad rhoi delweddau i lawr ar bapur neu ganfas yn unig oedd yr act o beintio llun, ond bod cariad a 'mood' yn rhan annatod o'r broses greadigol. Ymhlith ei athrawon yn y Slade roedd Randolph Schwabe (y Prifathro), Allan Gwynne-Jones a Tancred Borenius, arbenigwr ar gelfyddyd y Dadeni yn ardal Vicenza a Fenis yn yr Eidal. Er gwaethaf honiadau gwylaidd cyson Kyffin nad oedd ganddo dalent yn y cyfnod yma, dyfarnwyd ysgoloriaeth bwysig Robert Ross iddo pan adawodd y Slade.

Yn y pedwardegau, rhestrodd Kyffin Williams 'y gwŷr creadigol hynny oedd yn golygu llawer i mi'. Yn eu plith roedd Rembrandt a Vincent van Gogh. Soniodd lawer amdanynt. Dywedodd fod rhai peintiadau o eiddo Rembrandt yn gwneud iddo wylo, cymaint oedd yr emosiwn ynddynt. Gwelai debygrwydd rhwng bywyd Van Gogh a'i fywyd ei hun, Van Gogh yn fab i weinidog a Kyffin â chysylltiadau eglwysig niferus, a'r ddau ohonynt yn dioddef o epilepsi. Credai fod Van Gogh dan orfodaeth i gyfathrebu: 'Roedd rhaid iddo ddangos ei gariad at flodau neu bobl neu'r tirwedd, a dyna ni'. Felly hefyd Kyffin. Dywedodd droeon fod obsesiwn yn bwysicach na thalent, ond roedd Kyffin yn obsesiynol ac yn dalentog.

Ym 1944 penodwyd Kyffin i swydd athro celf hŷn yn Ysgol Highgate yn Llundain. Bu yno am gyfnod o naw mlynedd ar hugain, ei unig swydd ffurfiol fel athro, er iddo ledaenu gwybodaeth a rhannu o'i ddysg a'i ddawn gydol ei oes. Ym 1968 dyfarnwyd iddo Gymrodoriaeth Churchill i gofnodi y Gymdeithas Gymreig ym Mhatagonia. Dyma oedd antur fawr ei fywyd. Yn hanner cant oed, roedd yn awyddus i gyflawni rhywbeth arbennig. Bu yn y Wladfa am bedwar mis yn cofnodi y bobl, y tirwedd, yr adar a'r anifeiliaid. Dychwelodd i Gymru gyda chasgliad unigryw o beintiadau. Fe'i cyflwynodd yn rhodd i'r Llyfrgell Genedlaethol yn Aberystwyth, wedi i'r Amgueddfa

Genedlaethol ei wrthod. Ar sail ei rodd o gasgliad peintiadau Patagonia a'i roddion eraill, ystyrir Kyffin yn un o brif noddwyr y Llyfrgell Genedlaethol yn Aberystwyth. Bellach yn y Llyfrgell mae 700 o sleidiau lliw, lluniau camera a dynnwyd gan Kyffin yn y Wladfa, 250 o beintiadau olew (yn cynnwys Casgliad Patagonia) a 1,456 o weithiau creadigol ar bapur. Hwn yw'r casgliad mwyaf yn y byd o waith Kyffin. Yn ystod ei oes cyflwynodd rodd hefyd i Oriel Ynys Môn, sef 400 o luniau gwreiddiol o'i eiddo.

Ym Mai 1974 gadawodd ei swydd ddysgu yn Llundain a dychwelyd i Fôn, gan gael cartref iddo ei hun am y tro cyntaf yn ei fywyd, a hynny ym Mhwllfanogl ger pentref Llanfairpwllgwyngyll, mewn tŷ o eiddo Ardalydd ac Ardalyddes Môn, dau a fu'n noddwyr a chefnogwyr hael i Kyffin Williams. Ym Mhwllfanogl, o fewn tafliad carreg i'r Fenai, roedd Kyffin ym mharadwys, gyda mynyddoedd Eryri o'i flaen a thir ei hoff Sir Fôn dan ei draed. Yma bu ei gartref am weddill ei oes. Er ei fod yn byw yn hen lanc ar ei ben ei hun ym Mhwllfanogl, roedd ganddo gylch eang o gyfeillion a chydnabod.

Cyfrifir Kyffin Williams yn brif arlunydd Cymru a'r mwyaf llwyddiannus erioed o ran gyrfa fel artist proffesiynol. Gwnaeth ei lun cyntaf pan oedd oddeutu pedair oed, a pharhaodd i arlunio hyd ddiwedd ei oes hir. Adnabyddid ac edmygid ef gan lawer fel peintiwr mynyddoedd a'r môr oddiar arfordir Môn, ond yn ddiddorol, yn ei farn ei hun, o'i holl weithiau i'w rhoi ar bedastl, rhestrodd ddau beintiad o ffarmwr a'i gi mewn eira yn brwydro yn erbyn yr elfennau a dau bortread o ddwy wraig oedrannus. Ef am gyfnod oedd hoff bortreadwr sefydliadau Cymru gyda phrin yr un llywydd neu gadeirydd neu farnwr nas portreadwyd ganddo. Yn saith deg oed, cyhoeddodd ei ymddeoliad o'r dasg hon gan ddatgan na ddeuai'r gorchwyl yn hawdd iddo. Carai beintio blodau ac anifeiliaid, yn arbennig ceffylau a chŵn defaid. Un o ddoniau pennaf Kyffin Williams oedd y ddawn i 'osod' golygfa ar ganfas a'r gamp o wneud hynny drwy ddefnyddio cyllell balet yn hytrach na brwsh, yn wahanol iawn i'w gyfoeswyr. Carai beintio allan yn yr awyr agored ym mhob tywydd a pharhaodd i wneud hynny nes i ystyriaethau iechyd ei orfodi i'r stiwdio. Gweithiai yn gyflym iawn gan gwblhau portread mewn diwrnod.

Cynhaliodd ei arddangosfa gyntaf yn Oriel Colnaghi yn Llundain ym 1948 ac o 1975, am gyfnod o ddeng mlynedd ar hugain, bu'n cynnal arddangosfeydd yn Galeri y Thackeray yn yr un ddinas. Yng Nghymru bu'n arddangos yn gyson dros y blynyddoedd ym mhrif galerïau'r wlad. Dylid nodi yr arddangosfa adolygol gyntaf o'i waith yn yr Amgueddfa Genedlaethol yng Nghaerdydd, Mawrth 1987, arddangosfa o 131 o beintiadau. Gwelwyd yr arddangosfa hon yng Ngaleri y Glyn Vivian Abertawe ac hefyd yn Oriel Mostyn Llandudno. Dros y blynyddoedd bu nifer o arddangosfeydd cofiadwy o'i waith yn y Llyfrgell Genedlaethol yn Aberystwyth, un yn arbennig i ddathlu ei benblwydd yn 80 ar 9 Mai 1998, ac un arall i arddangos ei gasgliad Patagonia yn 2000. Cynhaliodd y Llyfrgell hefyd nifer o arddangosfeydd teithiol o'i waith. Bu Oriel Ynys Môn yn driw iawn iddo gan arddangos ei waith yn rheolaidd a chynnal dwy arddangosfa fawr o beintiadau - Arddangosfa Portreadau 1944-1991 ym 1993 ac Arddangosfa y Tirwedd ym 1995. Yn Oriel Ynys Môn hefyd y gwelwyd datblygu yr Oriel er cof am Kyffin Williams.

Bu nifer o galerïau yn gwerthu ei beintiadau, gyda thair yn cymeryd rhan amlwg yn y gweithgarwch, Galeri y Tegfryn ym Mhorthaethwy (er 1968), cyfeillion agos i Kyffin, Galeri y Thackeray yn Llundain (er 1975), noddwyr twymgalon, a Galeri yr Albany yng Nghaerdydd (er 1975). Gweithredai Mary Yapp, perchennog yr Albany, fel asiant iddo. Dylid nodi hefyd i Oriel Plas Glyn y Weddw Llanbedrog fod yn agos at galon Kyffin. Bellach mae ei waith celf mewn nifer o galerïau trwy Brydain a thramor, gyda'r mwyafrif o'r miloedd o luniau a beintiodd yn ystod ei oes mewn casgliadau preifat.

Yn ystod llwyddiannau Kyffin Williams yn y 1980au y lluniwyd y geiriau gogleisiol gan awdur anhysbys, 'Llwyddiant yw tŷ ym Mhontcanna, Volvo yn y garej a Kyffin ar y wal'. Yr oedd Kyffin bellach yn cynrychioli statws a'i beintiadau olew yn gwerthu am filoedd lawer. Symud o dlodi cymharol yn y pedwardegau i gyfoeth yn y nawdegau fu ei hanes. Yn ei ewyllys a luniwyd ym 1999, gadawodd filiynau o bunnoedd i'w rhannu rhwng ei deulu, cyfeillion agos a'r sefydliadau hynny a gefnogai, yn elusennau ac yn sefydliadau celfyddydol, megis Galeri y Tabernacl ym Machynlleth a'r cynllun mentrus i ddatblygu hen danerdy adfeiliedig yn y dref yn galeri gelf.

Yn ystod y deuddeng mlynedd ar hugain y bu'n byw ym Môn, pentyrrwyd pob anrhydedd arno: aelodaeth o'r Academi Frenhinol 1974, MA er anrhydedd Prifysgol Cymru 1978, Anrhydedd yr Ymerodraeth Brydeinig OBE 1983, Dirprwy Lifftenant Gwynedd 1987, cymrodoriaethau er anrhydedd Prifysgol Cymru Abertawe (1989), Prifysgol Cymru Bangor (1991) a Phrifysgol Cymru Aberystwyth (1992), Medal y Cymmrodorion 1991, Llywydd yr Academi Frenhinol Gymreig (am ddau gyfnod), Aelod o Lys Llyfrgell Genedlaethol Cymru, Gwobr Glyndŵr Ymddiriedolaeth y Tabernacl Machynlleth 1995, a'i urddo'n Farchog gan y Frenhines yn 1999.

Yn 2004, yn wythdeg chwech oed, teithiodd Kyffin Williams i ddinas Fenis ar gyfer rhaglen deledu wedi ei chomisiynu gan

BBC Cymru/Wales yn dwyn y teitl 'Reflections in a Gondola'. Cyfarwyddwyd y rhaglen hon gan John Hefin. Ynddi rhestrodd Kyffin bedwar digwyddiad arwyddocaol a thyngedfennol yn ei fywyd, sef ei eni yn Sir Fôn, gweld darlun o ffresco Piero della Francesca, peintio ar Gader Idris ym 1947 pryd y sylweddolodd y gallai efallai fod yn arlunydd, ac ymweld â Fenis am y tro cyntaf ym 1950, gan ryfeddu at ei champweithiau celfyddydol.

Cyhoeddodd Kyffin Williams ddwy gyfrol hunangofiannol, *Across the Straits* (1973) ac *A Wider Sky* (1991), cyfrolau a ystyrir yn glasuron o'u bath. Bu'n weithgar gyda Chymdeithas y Celfyddydau yng Ngogledd Cymru, a darlithiodd yn helaeth ar gelf led-led y wlad. Rhoddodd bob cymorth i ysgolion, gan groesawu dosbarthiadau di-ri i'w gartref a'i stiwdio ym Mhwllfanogl. Er y dywedai yn aml nad oedd am fod yn hen ŵr blin, safodd yn gadarn yn erbyn sothach ffansïol a elwid yn gelf gyfoes, hyd yn oed pan olygai hynny ymosodiadau arno yn y wasg. Mynnai barhau i amddiffyn y safonau gorau ym myd celf a pharchu traddodiad. Galwodd yn daer ar yr Amgueddfa Genedlaethol i arddangos Celf Cymru gyda'r pwyslais ar ddweud mai Cymry oedd yr artistiaid. Gresynodd na chafodd Richard Wilson ei gydnabod yn gall fel Cymro a John Gibson, y cerflunydd mawr o Gonwy yr un modd. Llafuriodd yn llwyddiannus gydag eraill i ddiogelu i Gymru gasgliad ei gyfaill, y peintiwr adar Charles Tunnicliffe, sail Oriel Ynys Môn.

Er i'w fam wahardd y Gymraeg ar yr aelwyd, a'r tad a'r fam yn siarad Cymraeg yn rhugl, siaradai Kyffin lawer o Gymraeg, gallai adrodd darnau o farddoniaeth Dafydd ap Gwilym, ysgrifennai at gyfeillion agos yn y Gymraeg, a phan ddatganodd yn yr wythdegau 'I paint in Welsh', golygai hyn ei fod wedi trechu tabŵ ei fam. Un o'i hoff eiriau yn ateb i'r cwestiwn "Sut ydech chi Kyffin?" oedd "O llipa", a'i hoff gyfarchiad pan yn arwyddo llyfrau fyddai 'Cofion Gorau - Kyffin'. Pan oedd ym Mhatagonia gorfu iddo ddarlledu ac annerch cynulleidfa yn y Gymraeg, profiad yn ôl ei dystiolaeth ei hun a wnaeth fyd o les iddo er gwella yr hyn a alwai ei 'Gymraeg coman'.

Dyn a'i draed ar y ddaear oedd Kyffin Williams, dyn ffraeth, llawn hiwmor a sgwrsiwr penigamp, gŵr hynod o wybodus am ei grefft a hanesydd celf heb ei ail. Gorfu iddo wynebu problemau dyrys yn ystod ei oes, iechyd ei frawd mawr Richard, cyfreithiwr galluog a ffefryn ei fam, a anafwyd yn ystod y rhyfel ac a aeth yn gaeth i'r ddiod, a'i iechyd ef ei hun, yr epilepsi a chancr y prostad a'r ysgyfaint - y cancr a'i lladdodd.

Bu farw yn 88 mlwydd oed yng Nghartref Sant Tysilio, Llanfairpwllgwyngyll, Ynys Môn, ar 1 Medi 2006, wedi cyfnod fel claf yn Ysbyty Gwynedd. Cynhaliwyd gwasanaeth angladdol ar 11 Medi yn Eglwys Gadeiriol Bangor, lle bu ei daid y Parchedig Owen Lloyd Williams yn ganghellor. Arweiniwyd y gwasanaeth gan Archesgob Cymru y Parchedicaf Barry Morgan, a chladdwyd Kyffin ym Mynwent Eglwys Llanfair-yng-Nghornwy, Môn, lle claddwyd ei daid. Cynlluniwyd ei garreg fedd gan ei gyfaill y cerflunydd Ieuan Rees, carreg seml a diarddurn o chwarel lechi Aberllefenni ym Meirionnydd. Ar 18 Gorffennaf 2008 agorwyd Oriel Kyffin Williams yn Llangefni yn gofadail urddasol iddo. Gweithia Ymddiriedolaeth Syr Kyffin Williams i hyrwyddo ei enw a hybu ei werthoedd ym myd celf.

Sir John Kyffin Williams
(1918 – 2006)

Kyffin Williams was born at Tanygraig, Llangefni, Anglesey, on 9 May 1918, the second son of Henry Inglis Wynne Williams (1870-1942), a bank manager, and his wife Essyllt Mary (1883-1964), daughter of Richard Hughes Williams, rector of Llansadwrn. Their first son, Owen Richard Inglis Williams (Dick), was born in 1916 and died in 1982. It was a matter of great pride for Kyffin Williams that his ancestral roots were deep in the land of Wales, in Anglesey (his father's family), in Montgomeryshire (where the name Kyffin came from) and in the vicinity of Strata Florida in Ceredigion (the burial place of his great-great-grandmother on his mother's side). On both sides of his family he was related to numerous Anglican clergymen and he admired their service to their fellow men. There were also some colourful individuals amongst his ancestors, such as Thomas Williams (1737-1802), the man who developed the copper industry at Parys Mountain in Anglesey.

After a short period in 1924 at Moreton Hall School near Chirk, where his father was a bank manager, Kyffin attended primary school at Trearddur Bay in Anglesey (1925-1931). Between 1931 and 1936 he was a boarder at Shrewsbury School, where he was unhappy due to loneliness and over-strict teachers. After he left school, his father arranged for him to join 'Yale and Hardcastle' land agents in Pwllheli (1937-1939), during which period he got to know the countryside of the Llŷn Peninsula from his home, by then in Abererch. At his mother's suggestion he joined Captain Jack Jones and the Ynysfor Hunt in the Aberglaslyn area, and he would roam the mountains in all weather, hunting foxes and exploring every nook and cranny, an invaluable experience for a landscape painter. It was said of Kyffin Williams that when he painted a mountain, he knew what was on the other side of the slope which faced him – he saw the full picture.

In 1937 he was commissioned as a Second Lieutenant in the Royal Welch Fusiliers (TA), but he was discharged from the army in 1940 after having an epileptic fit, a condition from which he suffered throughout his life. In this period he enjoyed the loyal companionship of Sandy Livingstone-Learmouth of Tremadog. It was Sandy who urged Kyffin to join the territorial army. The two had great fun composing 'Crawshaw-Bailey' limericks, comic verses to be sung to the tune of 'Mochyn Du'. The collection was published in *Boyo Ballads* (Excellent Press/National Library of Wales, 1995), a volume which displays Kyffin Williams's splendid cartoon work.

On his discharge from the army, the advice which Kyffin was given by the military doctor was: 'Williams, as you are in fact abnormal, I think it would be a good idea if you took up art', words which Kyffin took great delight in repeating when he was the grand old man of the arts in Wales. In October 1941 Kyffin enrolled as a student at the Slade School of Art, which had moved from London to the Ashmolean Museum in Oxford because of the war. Whilst gazing at a picture of Piero della Francesca's *Resurrection* in the Ashmolean, Kyffin experienced such an emotional response that he wept uncontrollably. As he recalled, this was his 'road to Damascus'. He realized for the first time that the act of painting a picture was not just a matter of placing images on paper or canvas, but that love and mood were essential aspects of the creative process. Amongst his teachers at the Slade were Randolph Schwabe (the Principal), Allan Gwynne-Jones and Tancred Borenius, a specialist on the Renaissance art of Vicenza and Venice in Italy. Despite Kyffin's constant self-deprecating claims that he had no talent in this period, he was awarded the prestigious Robert Ross scholarship when he left the Slade.

In the 1940s Kyffin Williams listed 'those creative men that meant much to me'. Amongst them were Rembrandt and Vincent van Gogh, about whom he had a great deal to say. He said that some paintings by Rembrandt contained so much emotion that they made him cry. He saw similarities between Van Gogh's life and his own, Van Gogh a pastor's son and Kyffin with his extensive church connections, and both afflicted by epilepsy. He believed that Van Gogh was compelled to express himself: 'He wanted to communicate, he just had to paint his love of things, be it flowers or people or landscape, and that was it'. So too Kyffin. He often claimed that obsession was more important than talent, but Kyffin was both obsessional and talented.

In 1944 he was appointed to the post of senior art master at Highgate School in London. He remained there for twenty-nine years, his only formal teaching post, although he spread knowledge and shared his learning and his gift throughout his life. In 1968 he was awarded the Churchill Fellowship to record the Welsh community in Patagonia. This was the greatest adventure of his life. Having reached the age of fifty, he was determined to accomplish something special. He stayed in the Welsh colony for four months, recording the people, the landscape, the birds and animals. He returned home with a unique and priceless collection of paintings. This he presented as a gift to the National Library in Aberystwyth, after the National Museum had refused it. On the basis of his collection of Patagonian paintings and other gifts, Kyffin is considered one of the main patrons of the National Library. By now the Library holds 700 colour slides, photographs taken by Kyffin in Patagonia, 250 oil paintings (including the Patagonian collection) and 1,456 creative works on paper. This is the largest collection in the world of Kyffin's work. During his lifetime he also presented 400 of his own paintings as a gift to Oriel Ynys Môn in Anglesey.

In May 1974 Kyffin left his teaching post in London and returned to Anglesey, where he made a home for himself for the first time in his life, at Pwllfanogl near the village of Llanfair Pwllgwyngyll, in a house which belonged to the Marquis and Marchioness of Anglesey, a couple who were generous patrons and supporters of Kyffin Williams. In Pwllfanogl, within a stone's throw of the Menai Straits, Kyffin was in paradise, with the mountains of Snowdonia in front of him and the earth of his beloved Anglesey beneath his feet. This was to be his home for the rest of his life. Although he lived a bachelor existence in Pwllfanogl, he had a wide circle of friends and acquaintances.

Kyffin Williams is considered to be Wales's foremost painter and the most successful ever in terms of his career as a professional artist. He was about four years old when he painted his first picture, and he continued to paint until the end of his long life. He was known and admired by many as a painter of the mountains and the sea off the coast of Anglesey, but interestingly, in his own opinion, of all his works to put on a pedestal, he selected two paintings of a farmer and his dog in snow battling against the elements and two portaits of two old ladies. For a time he was the portrait artist of choice for Welsh institutions, with hardly a president or chairman or judge whose portrait he did not paint. At the age of seventy he announced his retirement from this task, saying that such work did not come easily to him. He loved to paint flowers and animals, particularly horses and sheepdogs. One of Kyffin Williams's greatest gifts was the ability to 'set' a scene on canvas, which he did using a pallet knife rather than a brush, a technique quite different to that of his contemporaries. He liked to paint in the open air in all weathers, and he continued to do so until health considerations forced him into the studio. He worked very quickly, finishing a portrait in a day.

He held his first exhibition at the Colnaghi Gallery in London in 1948, and for a period of thirty years from 1975 he held exhibitions at the Thackeray Gallery in the same city. In Wales, he exhibited regularly over the years in the main galleries. The first retrospective exhibition of his work, consisting of 131 paintings, was held at the National Museum in Cardiff in March 1987, an exhibition which was also seen at the Glyn Vivian Gallery in Swansea and at Oriel Mostyn in Llandudno. A number of memorable exhibitions of his work were held at the National Library in Aberystwyth, one in particular to celebrate his eightieth birthday on 9 May 1998, and another to display his Patagonian collection in 2000. The Library also put on several travelling exhibitions of his work. Oriel Ynys Môn was also very loyal, showing his work regularly and holding two major exhibitions of paintings - Portraits 1944-1991 in 1993 and Landscapes in 1995. And it was in Oriel Ynys Môn that the Kyffin Williams memorial gallery was established.

A number of galleries sold his paintings, and three were particularly prominent: the Tegfryn Gallery in Menai Bridge (since 1968), close friends of Kyffin, the Thackeray Gallery in London (since 1975), enthusiastic supporters, and the Albany Gallery in Cardiff (since 1975). Mary Yapp, the owner of the Albany, acted as his agent. Oriel Plas Glyn y Weddw in Llanbedrog was also very close to Kyffin's heart. His work is now in many galleries throughout Britain and overseas, with the majority of the thousands of pictures which he painted during his lifetime in private collections.

The prestige of Kyffin Williams's work by the 1980s led an unknown wag to claim that 'success is a house in Pontcanna, a Volvo in the garage and a Kyffin on the wall'. By then Kyffin represented status, and his oil paintings sold for many thousands. Having begun his career in comparative poverty in the forties, by the nineties he was a wealthy man. In his will, which was drawn up in 1999, he left millions of pounds to be shared between his family, close friends and those institutions which he supported, charities and arts bodies, such as the Tabernacle Gallery in Machynlleth and the bold scheme to develop a ruined tannery in the town into an art gallery.

During the thirty-two years that he lived in Anglesey, honours were heaped upon him: membership of the Royal Academy (1974), honorary MA from the University of Wales (1978), an OBE (1983), the title of Deputy Lieutenant of Gwynedd (1987), honorary fellowships from the University of Wales Swansea (1989), the University of Wales Bangor (1991) and the University of Wales Aberystwyth (1992), the Cymmrodorion medal (1991), the title of President of the Royal Cambrian Academy (for two periods), membership of the Court of the National Library of Wales, the Glyndŵr Award of the Tabernacle Trust, Machynlleth (1995), and a knighthood in 1999.

In 2004, at the age of eighty-six, Kyffin Williams travelled to Venice for a television programme commissioned by BBC Cymru/Wales, directed by John Hefin and entitled '*Reflections in a Gondola*'. In it Kyffin listed the four most significant and fateful events of his life: his birth in Anglesey, seeing the picture of the fresco by Piero della Francesca, painting on Cader Idris in 1947 when he first realized that he could perhaps become an artist, and visiting Venice for the first time in 1950, when he marvelled at its artistic masterpieces.

Kyffin Williams published two volumes of autobiography, *Across the Straits* (1973) and *A Wider Sky* (1991), both of which are considered classics of their kind. He was active with the North Wales Arts Association, and lectured extensively on art throughout the country. He gave every support to schools, welcoming countless classes into his home and studio in Pwllfanogl. Although he often said that he did not want to be a grumpy old man, he stood firm against the 'fanciful rubbish' called modern art, even when that led to attacks upon him in the press. He was determined to defend the highest standards in art and to respect tradition. He urged the National Museum to exhibit Welsh art and to emphasise that the artists were Welsh. It annoyed him that Richard Wilson had not been properly recognised as a Welshman, and likewise John Gibson, the great sculptor from Conway. He and others worked hard to preserve for Wales the collection of his friend, the bird artist Charles Tunnicliffe, which was the basis of the Oriel Ynys Môn art gallery.

Although his mother would allow no Welsh to be spoken in the home, his parents were both fluent Welsh speakers, and Kyffin himself spoke a good deal of Welsh, being able to recite passages of poetry by Dafydd ap Gwilym, and he used to write to his close friends in Welsh. When Kyffin declared in the 1980s 'I paint in Welsh', this meant that he had overcome his mother's taboo. When signing books, his favourite greeting was 'Cofion Gorau - Kyffin'. During his stay in Patagonia he had to broadcast and address audiences in Welsh, an experience which, according to his own testimony, did a great deal to improve what he called his 'common Welsh'.

Kyffin Williams had his feet firmly on the ground; he was eloquent, full of humour and a wonderful conversationalist, extremely knowledgeable about his craft and an art historian second to none. He had to deal with difficult problems during his life: the health of his older brother Richard, an able lawyer and his mother's favourite, who was wounded during the war and became an alcoholic, and his own health, the epilepsy and cancer of the prostate and of the lung - the cancer which killed him.

He died at the age of 88 in the St Tysilio Home, Llanfair Pwllgwyngyll, Anglesey, on 1 September 2006, after a period of illness in Ysbyty Gwynedd. His funeral service was held on 11 September in Bangor Cathedral, where his grandfather the Reverend Owen Lloyd Williams had been chancellor. The service was led by the Archbishop of Wales, the Most Reverend Barry Morgan, and Kyffin was buried in the cemetery of Llanfair-yng-Nghornwy Church, Anglesey, where his grandfather was buried. His gravestone was designed by his friend the sculptor Ieuan Rees, a simple unadorned stone from the Aberllefenni slate quarry in Meirionethshire. On 18 July 2008 Oriel Kyffin Williams was opened in Llangefni as a fitting memorial to him. The Sir Kyffin Williams Trust works to promote his name and his values in the art world.

Kyffin Williams: The Portraits

Peter Lord

In preparing to write this lecture I accumulated a large – and ultimately rather intimidating – quantity of notes, representing thoughts on various aspects of the life and work of Kyffin Williams. There were far too many to fit into an hour's discussion and they ranged much more widely than the place of the portraits in his output. As a result, increasingly I felt that I could not approach that particular group of pictures without reaching first for some degree of clarity about other aspects of a life's work that, in fact, I have found extremely difficult to grasp. It was as if the notes that I had made were pieces of a jigsaw that refused to come together to form a single picture. After reading everything that Kyffin wrote for publication, many of his letters, and most of the observations made about him by other people, I found myself at the end, as at the beginning, faced with the problem of writing about a man whom I can only describe as an enigma – and, I suspect, a man who was an enigma to himself, as much as he was to the rest of us.

The fundamental problem was how to differentiate between the paintings of Kyffin Williams and the phenomenon of Kyffin Williams – that is to say, the unusual place of this artist in public consciousness, signified firstly, of course, by the fact that we almost always refer to him simply by his Christian name. I considered what might be the effect on you of what I said today if I chose to refer to him always as 'Williams', rather than as Kyffin – what would that signal to you? Perhaps pretentiousness, perhaps hostility? The second obvious indicator of an unusual relationship between the paintings and the phenomenon is the market value of his work. In their summary of business during 2017, the auctioneers Rogers Jones noted the ten top prices paid for Welsh art. The first seven pictures on the list were all painted by Kyffin. However, the relationship between the pictures and this remarkable market dominance of a single painter is not necessarily as direct as one might expect. An historical comparison might be helpful here.

The only visual artist of the past who can claim an equivalent place in the public domain in Wales to that taken by Kyffin Williams is Richard Wilson. Curiously, there are parallels between the painters not only in terms of their public profile, but also in the nature of their practice. Like Kyffin, Wilson's reputation became so focused on his landscape painting that the twenty years that he spent training in London and practising as a portrait painter have largely been ignored. But Wilson did indeed paint portraits of a substantial number of gentlemen and ladies, just as Kyffin painted portraits of leading establishment figures in his time. Wilson was a founder of the Royal Academy, of course, membership of which would subsequently be so important to Kyffin – indeed, as he said once, with a characteristic degree of hyperbole, 'the only thing of any importance really that ever happened to me in my life.'[1] Again, the commercial success of both artists spawned imitators and, indeed, created an opening for forgers because the style of their work was so distinctive. However, the parallel to which I want to draw most attention concerns the fact that in the mind of the public, both painters came to represent something beyond the aesthetics of their pictures, something that had meaning for people who might never have seen an original, never mind owned one. In a book that I published some years ago, called *Richard Wilson: Life and Legacy*, I made the point that it was *the idea* of Richard Wilson, rather than the quality of his pictures, that had the most lasting influence in Wales itself. For Welsh people, especially in the aspirational later nineteenth century, the life of Richard Wilson became a metaphor for a story about their country. Wilson came to represent the potential of an awakening nation. A mythology developed around him in which he was presented as rising from humble origins (which he did not), of progressing in London against the hostility of the English (embodied in the person of Joshua Reynolds, the evil genius of the narrative), of his passionate and poetic Celtic nature (contrasted against the cerebral cool of the English psyche), and so on and so forth. Against all the odds, Wilson had triumphed and became the greatest landscape painter in England – indeed, the founder of the 'English School'. Much of this was far removed from the facts

---

[1] British Library, National Life Stories: Artists' Lives: Kyffin Williams, C466/24, interview with Cathy Courtney (1995), p. 148.

of his career development and the aesthetics of his pictures. Now the particular details of what Kyffin Williams came to represent in Wales were not the same as those which were represented by Richard Wilson, because the needs of their two periods were different, but there was a parallel in the disconnect that developed between the reality of the pictures and what the totality of the narrative signified in the public mind. As with Wilson in the late eighteenth and the nineteenth centuries, to buy a Kyffin in the twentieth- or twenty-first centuries is not so much to purchase a painting, as to purchase an idea.

A parallel between Kyffin Williams and his contemporary painter John Elwyn is also instructive. The careers of the two men began equally auspiciously, and indeed they shared at least one early patron, Winifred Coombe Tennant. She had first seen John Elwyn's work in 1947, and soon afterwards bought pictures both for herself and for the Glynn Vivian Art Gallery, for whom she acted in London. She bought her first Kyffin landscape in 1950. By the time of her death in 1956 she had acquired five of his oils and a group of watercolours, and six oil landscapes by John Elwyn. Coombe Tennant's reaction to Kyffin's work is worth noting for its conviction that here she had found something special. In November of that year she visited his studio – 'a dreary room in Bisham Gardens in Highgate Village', as he described it:[2]

> Started in dense fog at 10 a.m. for Highgate to see Kyffin Williams' pictures in Hampstead. Visibility almost nil, we crawled on and, finally, came to the house. Saw some 30 or 40 pictures, many of them fine. I bought one, a dark North

---

[2] 'Kyffin Williams' in *Artists in Wales*, ed. Meic Stephens (Llandysul, 1971), p. 17.

Wales mountains, with a lake in the foreground – for £25. A superb painting. Kyffin, small, emaciated (tb), and entirely delightful, much interesting talk. The two pictures he is sending to the Leicester Gallery soon, very fine, especially one of Hafod Fawr, [sic] Festiniog Mountains – farmstead and fields – but I liked my picture best of all, very North Wales of very North Wales. Drove slowly through the fog past Highgate Cemetery, where is an empty tomb.[3]

Winifred was also buying the pictures of J.D. Innes at this time, and was much attracted to the idea of the tragic young visionary – hence the TB, the smog, the empty tomb and, perhaps, the choice of *Llynau Cwm Silyn*, a pretty mournful place to paint at the best of times. Winifred shared the twin loves of Kyffin, the mountains and the sea, and her next purchase was an early interpretation of a theme to which he would return periodically until the end of his life, *The Wave*. She saw the picture at the Leicester Galleries and, on this occasion, chose Kyffin over John Elwyn, also exhibiting there. She had recently seen the work of both painters together at a seminal exhibition at the Caerphilly National Eisteddfod:

...saw two John Elwyns, better than those at Caerphilly, and saw two superb Kyffin Williams, one of which I felt I couldn't live without. 'The Wave', a seascape, 30 guineas ... I saw some lovely pictures in the gallery, but 'The Wave' exceeded them all ... my heart fills with joy when I think of 'The Wave'.[4]

---

[3] NLW, Diary of Winifred Coombe Tennant, 26 November 1950.
[4] Ibid., 14 August 1950

Coombe Tennant admired the work of both painters, and as a patriot who had inherited the spirit of the late nineteenth- and early twentieth-century national revival, she was excited also by what the emergence of work of this quality and relevance represented for Wales. However, her relationship with the two men developed in a significantly different way. Kyffin replied to Winifred's letters with brief cheery notes, written in the large round hand that remained characteristic of his epistles till the end. For instance, from Menai Bridge he wrote:

> Am up here for a holiday – no painting but a few days hunting. Am off to Penygwryd tomorrow to hunt on the Glyders. Shall take a sketch book and make notes.[5]

Coombe Tennant's letters to John Elwyn elicited a very different response – long, detailed observations on art and on the development of his career. John Elwyn's letters were thoughtful and serious, whereas Kyffin's were all cheery surface, revealing nothing of his inner world.

Nevertheless, in 1950, Coombe Tennant rightly thought that both painters, to use a phrase of her own, were 'the real thing'. So why is it that the huge output of elegant pictures of Welsh landscape painted by John Elwyn, popular as they would become with collectors, do not now have nearly the same value in the art market as the works of Kyffin Williams? As a rule, I'm not interested in making relative evaluations of the aesthetic quality of the work of painters, because I don't find it enlightening in terms of understanding the wider cultural issues that paintings reflect.

---

[5] NLW Winifred Coombe Tennant, artists' correspondence, letter from Kyffin Williams, 3 December 1954.

Nevertheless, if I were to venture into that area, I think it would be difficult to argue that pictures painted by Kyffin Williams are, in terms of quality, the quantum leap ahead of those painted by John Elwyn that would be suggested by their market value and by the public awareness of the artist. This is not a comparison rendered problematic on the grounds that one is comparing chalk with cheese, since the painters were contemporaries, and both remained committed to the craft of the figurative tradition throughout their careers. Both were concerned primarily with imaging Welsh rural landscapes and the inhabitants of those landscapes, and both strongly referenced passing or passed ways of life. How is it, then, that the one died plain John Elwyn and the other, Sir John Kyffin Williams KBE RA? Was there, perhaps, something in the development of their work, after the death of Coombe Tennant, that accounts for the difference?

When in doubt, one usually foolproof way to construct a lecture about an elusive visual artist is to flesh out the discussion on the basis of a skeletal structure that follows the evolution of the work through his or her career. That will not serve in the case of Kyffin Williams, whose work over his long lifetime did not in any fundamental sense evolve from that bought by Winifred Coombe Tennant in the 1950s. Certainly if we look at the landscapes which constitute the bulk of his vast output, in essence they change little in technique or content from the point at which, very early on, he established his method of painting with a palette knife. In fact, one possible reason for this lack of evolution is to be found in his adherence to that constraining technique – along with his adherence also to his core subject matter, of course. This lack of evolution applies to his drawing and to his watercolours as much as to his oils. Kyffin indeed acknowledged it, though he felt that his work had improved over the years: 'I have improved out of all recognition', he remarked, late in life, though that was not a conclusion with which many critics would concur, since the early work and the late work is indeed immediately recognisable as the product of the same hand.[6]

Kyffin Williams chose to explain his consistency in terms of 'obsession'. Another way of looking at it might be to suggest that he had a fear of venturing outside his comfort zone. Indeed, in the narrative of his life which he assiduously constructed through his writings and interviews, Kyffin himself provided a good deal of evidence to support this interpretation. He liked to describe himself as having no talent. Of course, at the same time, he made it clear that in his opinion talent was a greatly over-valued commodity:

> Now I didn't particularly want to take up art. I suppose I didn't think I had the talent, and talent you know is a totally worthless thing. I believe what is important is obsession … And I have the obsession because of my background …[7]

He was, he said, a painter who came to art by accident – by 'amazing good fortune' – but from the start he seems to have been fundamentally insecure about the whole project.[8] He acknowledged an inner uncertainty that, like so many other aspects of his personality, seems contradictory because, at a superficial level at any rate, his mastery of his chosen technique suggests nothing if not a supremely confident artist. Even

---

[6] BL National Life Stories, p. 66.
[7] Ibid., p. 68.
[8] Stephens, p. 10.

in the late 1950s and through the 1960s, when many of his contemporaries were blown off course by the huge weight of art-world fashion for non-figurative painting, it is difficult to detect any response in Kyffin's work. In the pictures of John Elwyn, perhaps his most consistent contemporary, it is easy to see in the geometric formalisation and patterning of paintings produced in the late 1950s and 1960s a move towards a compromise position, and though it was expressed in a different way, the same non-figurative influence appeared in the work of Gwilym Prichard at that time. Some contemporaries, notably Heinz Koppel, abandoned figurative painting altogether. Kyffin did acknowledge the pressure to walk the non-figurative party line. In a 1961 catalogue essay he said this:

> At the moment I am trying to get greater breadth into my paintings and I suppose they are becoming more abstract, but I reckon I like landscapes and people too much to paint real abstracts.[9]

In time, of course, this rather mild expression of Kyffin's attitude to what he called, in the popular shorthand of the period, 'abstracts', would harden, and indeed his hostility to non-figurative art became an important element in defining his public persona. It went down well with the general public, who were pleased to identify with an expert spokesperson who voiced their antipathy to forms of art to with which they were unsympathetic. This had the effect of turning Kyffin into a

---

[9] *Jonah Jones; John Petts; Kyffin Williams* (1961) given in David Meredith and John Smith, *Obsessed. The Biography of Kyffin Williams* (Llandysul, 2012), p. 110.

sort of Nigel Farage of the art world, to whom the press could always turn for a provocative quote. The inevitable polarising consequence was that the art establishment in Wales, deeply invested in the non-figurative fashion, soon elevated him to the position of honorary chief spokesperson for the reactionary tendency, and slighted his pictures largely on principle. Because of Kyffin's fundamental insecurity about his work, this reaction resulted in the quite disproportionate concern that he developed about what he presented as his victimisation by the Welsh art world. I think it fair to say that this concern approached the level of a persecution complex, and the intensity with which he voiced it in a long interview recorded in 1995 for the British Library's 'National Life Stories' project, is surely a measure of the depth of his insecurity as a painter:

> But in the art world now, I mean they think absolutely nothing of my work, nothing at all, and in Wales, the art establishment in Wales, they think nothing of my work. I'm a danger … the director of the North Wales Association of the Arts told me he heard the director of the Welsh Arts Council and the Director of Art at the Welsh Arts Council agreeing that I was the greatest single danger to Welsh art …' [10]

In the same interview, Kyffin alleged that his portrait book was 'blocked by the Welsh Arts Council.' This was his way of saying that they didn't grant-aid it – along with the projects of dozens of other artists, of course, not mentioned.

In fact, this complex was the reason that I first became aware of Kyffin Williams. I arrived in Wales in the same year, 1974,

---

[10] BL National Life Stories, p. 65.

that the painter gave up his day job in Highgate and came home. Kyffin was often in the news over the next few years complaining about the lack of patronage in Wales and how difficult it was to earn a living here as an artist. Unaware of the background, at first this attitude simply puzzled me but soon it began to seem quite absurd, because my experience on the ground was that just about every house that I entered that was owned by middle-class people with an interest in art, especially if they were Welsh-speaking, contained a picture referred to as 'our Kyffin'. But the polarity of opinion about his work persists, and it is still regarded by many in the art world, and especially, I notice, by other artists, with disdain. For some, it may be an opinion about the quality of the work itself, or the commercial success of the work and the resultant status of the painter, that is the source of the resentment – but I suspect that, for most, the negative reaction to Kyffin Williams is rooted in something deeper and more visceral.

There is a curious anecdote worth adding here, apropos of Kyffin's attitude to non-figurative painting. While he was on his travels, soon after the Second World War, he met in Rome a young Yugoslav painter called Albert Alcalay, newly released from an Italian internment camp. They exchanged portraits of each other and became friends – indeed, one of Alcalay's two portraits of Kyffin is signed with an affectionate inscription. Kyffin chose to include his portrait of Alcalay in the volume *Portraits* – but in his accompanying text he omitted the sequel to the story of their brief acquaintance. In 1951, Alcalay would leave Rome for the United States, where he became a high-profile and successful proponent of non-figurative painting.

It appears then, that with the exception of the first tentative years, it is not enlightening to approach Kyffin by writing about his work in terms of evolution. A second possible approach – a straightforward biographical account, tracking his movements, the people he met and so forth – seems equally limited in potential, since he wrote extensively on these matters himself, apparently answering all the questions one might want to ask. There would appear to be little of a factual, biographical nature, that one can usefully add which might prove revealing of aspects of the painter's sources and intentions. His own writings were designed, it would seem, to leave no-one in any doubt about who was Kyffin Williams.

And yet, to my mind, the sheer quantity of these autobiographical writings, along with the interviews he gave and the television films in which he participated, raise interesting issues about Kyffin Williams' sense of himself, and therefore about his paintings and, indeed, people's reactions to them. As a part of the preparation of this lecture I inspected all the work that Kyffin bequeathed as an archive to the National Library. He left hundreds of watercolours and drawings, all now immaculately mounted and conserved – and what is most striking about the collection, considered as a whole, is the absence within it of those revealing failures, those inconsequential notes, those speculative thoughts and questions scribbled on the side or the back of a drawing, those torn scraps, that characterise the archives of just about every other artist that I have ever inspected. The Kyffin archive has been comprehensively filleted and sanitised. In fact, I have to admit that I found the bland uniformity of this vast collection rather depressing – box after box full of clean, inoffensive landscapes, portraits of pretty children, sheepdogs and farm animals, nearly all tidily initialled, and with only the very occasional sheet that revealed a more intense vision or signs that there had been a struggle to resolve the image. After a day in the stacks at the National Library, I began to wonder if that standard criticism made by those people unsympathetic to Kyffin's work, 'Seen one, seen the lot', was not as trite as it usually sounds. It would seem that Kyffin Williams' need to define his identity thoroughly and unequivocally in words also extended to the work itself – that he was determined to exercise a degree of control over his legacy that has had the effect of concealing the vulnerability of the maker. We know that Kyffin also destroyed any oil paintings that he considered not up to scratch. His own word – 'obsession' – once again comes to mind. Kyffin seems to have been obsessed with creating a clearly defined image of himself, with no loose ends – which suggests to me the degree to which he was troubled by the many loose ends, the many uncertainties, to which he only alludes in passing in the entertaining anecdotal flow of his writing. 'There have been unhappy moments in my life', he recalled, 'but I see no reason for dredging them from the mental congestion in my own personal bucket. When I look back on my life the glories of past summers are more memorable than the storms …'[11] Somehow, one rather doubts it. 'Tragedy to me is a far more potent force than joy', he observed on another occasion.[12]

The emotional uncertainties that lie suppressed beneath the assertiveness and the technical authority of Kyffin Williams' landscape painting and its most characteristic subject matter – the mountains of Snowdonia – present in personal microcosm a cultural reality that, I think, in large measure accounts for the Kyffin phenomenon. The pictures present a construct of

---

[11] Kyffin Williams, *A Wider Sky* (Llandysul, 1991), p. xiv. Nevertheless, Williams then proceeds to the story of his unrequited love for Susan Kyffin.
[12] BL National Life Stories, p. 125.

national identity that seems clear and uncompromised. The physical permanence of the mountains of Snowdonia has long been exploited as a metaphor for the underlying durability of the Welsh people. The notion was deployed most explicitly in the nineteenth- and early twentieth-century nationalism of O.M. Edwards and Tom Ellis, and in the literature and visual art of their contemporaries. Edwards' *Hanes Cymru i Ysgolion*, published in 1911 at the peak of the revival of national cultural assertiveness, opens with a painting by Samuel Maurice Jones. *Eryri* was not presented as a topographical illustration but as the primary symbol of the soul of the nation that Edwards voiced in all his writing and publishing. The landscape imagery of Kyffin Williams has resonated deeply with generations of the Welsh public – especially the Welsh-speaking public – who remain in touch with that tradition of political and artistic thinking, but who have lived, in our time, in a day-to-day world almost every aspect of which proclaims a different reality. In an increasingly confused and conflicted Welsh twentieth century (and into the present), the Kyffin Williams landscape has offered a link to the imagined certainties of the romantic nationalism that was mortally wounded by the Great War. Kyffin's recourse in his written and spoken language to antiquated notions of Welsh ethnicity, his references to the 'my Celtic imagination', 'a typical north Wales Celt', and to the 'the natural characteristics of the Welshman', underline the degree to which his vision was rooted in that cultural inheritance.[13] Inside the four walls of the houses where his pictures are so highly valued, his oil landscapes, watercolours and prints bolster a sense of identity

---

[13] Kyffin Williams, *Portraits* (Llandysul, 1996), pp. 18 and 80. Nicholas Sinclair, *Kyffin Williams* (Lund Humphries, 2004) p. 112.

profoundly challenged the minute his patrons step outside into the discontinuity of the Wales of the present.

In historical terms, this is why the phenomenon of Kyffin Williams is important. Whether or not his pictures exemplify 'good art' is not the issue. The level of public engagement with what his work represents, whether loyal or hostile – and there is little in between – indicates the nation's crisis of identity, which is to say, in our time, no less than the nation's crisis of existence. The phenomenon of Kyffin Williams reflects a disrupted relationship between an idea of Wales and the homogenised global reality that has all but consumed it. As I suggested earlier, it seems to me that ownership of a picture by Kyffin Williams indicates something essentially different from ownership of, say, a picture by Donald McIntyre. It is not an expression of a straightforward attraction to an artist's rendition of a landscape, but of allegiance to an idea – to what that landscape represents to a Welsh cultural consciousness. The gloom of so many of the pictures reflects the fact that this consciousness has, of course, been under threat of assimilation over many centuries, effected through political structures, through industrialisation, through de-industrialisation, through inward migration and through language change. But Kyffin's period marked the endgame, hence the intensity of feeling that the work aroused and continues to arouse, on both sides. It is significant that Kyffin embarked on his public career with his first exhibition in the same year – 1948 – as that other great work of resistant ruralist Welsh identity, Iorwerth Peate's Sain Ffagan, was created. R.S. Thomas's elegy to cultural decay, *The Stones of the Field*, had been published two years earlier, in 1946, and in 1949, Geoff Charles' and John Roberts Williams' film, *Yr Etifeddiaeth*, was made – a film that concludes with the truly

Kyffinesque image of the sun setting into a grey and empty sea, extending unbroken from one side of the frame – the canvas – to the other.

Ironically, it was precisely Kyffin's initial alignment with the prevailing intellectual mood in Wales in the 1940s and early 1950s that would lead, before long, to the art world outsiderness which so troubled him for the rest of his life. The enthusiasm with which his work had been received by well-placed early patrons such as Winifred Coombe Tennant suggested that all was set fair. Kyffin stood in the mainstream of a national zeitgeist, manifested in visual art by what critics defined as 'Welsh Environmentalism'. It was a movement characterised by 'love and compassion for humanity and a consciousness of the relation of men and women to nature, buildings and everyday life in Wales', as the painter and administrator John Petts had put it in 1953, in the catalogue to the exhibition 'Contemporary Welsh Painting and Sculpture'. Introducing a follow-up travelling exhibition the following year, Saunders Lewis remarked, more simply, that the pictures 'tell us about Wales'.[14] Welsh Environmentalism was not an artist-led concept, but rather a critical response to the works of painters like Kyffin, John Elwyn, Ernest Zobole and Brenda Chamberlain and, indeed, to some artists who had come to work in Wales from outside, notably Josef Herman and Heinz Koppel. These painters seemed to critics to share an ethos that reflected a prevailing mood. It was in this context that David Bell, in his book *The Artist in Wales*, published the first extended notice of Kyffin. However, just at the moment at which Bell's exposition of the work appeared in 1957, the context changed

---

[14] See Peter Lord, *The Tradition: a New History of Welsh Art, 1400–1990* (Cardigan, 2016), p. 339.

radically. The year before the publication of *The Artist in Wales* saw the establishment of the 56 Group, which although it initially included some of Kyffin's figurative painter contemporaries, was driven by young practitioners committed to internationalist non-figurative art. One of the leading lights, David Tinker, was quoted in that foundation year as being opposed to 'the prosaic, environment-ridden style of painting he sees done by Welsh artists' – artists like Kyffin Williams, who was not invited to join the group.[15] The 56 Group was promoted enthusiastically by the Arts Council, which had already assumed by that time the leading position that it occupied in the Welsh art world into the 1980s, dominating public patronage and setting the intellectual tone in cahoots with the expanding art colleges, in which most of the non-figurative artists worked.

From the second half of the 1950s, the immediate post-war mainstream was relegated to the reactionary sidelines – though Kyffin sometimes found himself in a somewhat odd position, caught between the two. Crusty conservatives, whose portraits he was called upon to paint, especially individuals whose genealogical credentials were as impeccable as his own, continued to express their distaste for his pictures on the grounds of their modernism. As late as 1970 he wrote to a friend that:

> My portrait for the Caernarvonshire magistrates of Lord Morris of Borth y Gest was rejected unanimously, one elderly gentleman saying it would make 'damn good target practice for the T.A.'[16]

---

[15] Goronwy Powell in the *Western Mail*, 27 January 1956.
[16] NLW Jack Raymond Jones Papers, letter to Jack Jones dated 21 August 1970.

Kyffin's frequently-voiced complaint about his outsider status in the Welsh art world of the 1960s and 70s was characterised by the suggestion that his rejection was unique and personal. This was quite untrue, and surely an expression of those uncertainties whose roots lay elsewhere – a convenient focus for a broader personal angst. In fact, Kyffin's position was typical of all those artists who did not succumb to the new internationalist fashion – an impressive list including Zobole and Prichard, Vera Bassett, Claudia Williams, Joan Baker and many others. The only unique characteristic of the comparable marginalisation of the work of Kyffin Williams was the volume of the fuss he made about it. M.E. Eldridge presents a striking parallel. It was in the foundation year of the 56 Group that she completed, after years of dedicated labour, the most ambitious figurative composition painted in Wales in the years after the Second World War, *The Dance of Life*. The completion in 1956 of Eldridge's remarkable mural sequence went un-noticed in this country, a victim of the change in aesthetic fashion. Only privately, in her autobiographical journal, written in old age, did Eldridge express her resentment about the direction in which things had moved in the art world in the decade after the war, though she saw it through an anti-democratic lens:

> People became all important. Everyone painted, everyone wrote poetry, everyone produced a book to express their important selves – scarcely a good painting, poem or other to be seen. People expressing their mostly unpleasant selves.[17]

---

[17] Autobiographical Journal, Bangor University Archives, p. 207.

At almost the same time as Eldridge was writing in private, Kyffin gave public vent to his parallel frustration at what had happened after the war with an outburst of anti-intellectualism expressed in his autobiographical interview for the British Library:

> … after the Second World War, I believe that a lot of woolly individuals, woolly intellectuals, got together and said, 'We are now moving into the 21st century, a century of robots and computers, and by God we've got to create the art of the 21st century to go with the computers and the robots. And of course we cannot do that until we … destroy tradition. Tradition is what's holding back the future of art …'[18]

But the distaste expressed in some quarters in Wales for Kyffin's pictures was never simply an aspect of the debate between proponents of figurative and non-figurative art, which was an argument underway throughout Britain. The debate in this country differed from that over the border, where – notwithstanding the persistent strand of English Neo-Romanticism – the aesthetic context had been more diverse since the 1930s. In Wales, the critical understanding of our post-war art as representing a very particular Welsh-*ness* gave a sharp contentious edge to the argument. As the falling away of people such as Will Roberts from the hard core of the 56 Group soon made clear, many of the proponents of the new way, notably Tinker, Robert Hunter, and Tom Hudson, were English outsiders who felt personally threatened, indeed, alienated in the strict sense of the word, by the strong cultural identification of post-war Welsh painting.

---

[18] BL National Life Stories, p. 88.

That said, it is clear that the cultural resonance of Kyffin's pictures also represented a challenge to insiders with a different Welsh identity – individuals who took exception to the sense that in some way images redolent of an unchanging pre-industrial culture, closely associated with a language they did not speak and portraying a geography with which they were unfamiliar, were presumed by others to be the unique embodiment of the nation. Their irritation has been increased by the perceptions of some English writers about the work and what it implied about Wales. Nicholas Sinclair believed that Kyffin 'was able to express a profound truth about his native land which no other Welsh painter has yet achieved. It is for this reason that Williams is now recognised as the artist whose work defines the spirit of Wales.'[19] Kyffin himself fed this perception, with more than one reference to 'the South', as if it were a foreign country. Furthermore, in the 1980s, dissenting opinions were voiced by some who, although themselves in touch with the nineteenth-century romantic nationalist tradition, in particular through language, felt that Kyffin's pictures did nothing to engage with the present realities of threatened, if conflicted, Welsh identities that it was the responsibility of the socially and politically engaged artist to face.

Kyffin did retain supporters among his fellow practitioners, including Jack Jones, with whom he developed a close relationship, visiting him on occasions in Swansea. Jones was a painter who might have been expected to dislike his pictures, given his working-class origins in urban industrial Wales, but there must be many people who wish that they had taken his advice, offered in a prescient review of Kyffin's work in 1966:

---

[19] Rian Evans and Nicholas Sinclair, *The Art of Kyffin Williams* (London, 2007) p. 31.

The drawings and paintings which sell at from 30 guineas up are an excellent investment of anybody's money. One day, when all the hysteria of pop-art, junk-art, plastic sculpture and the rest has died down, there will be a re-valuation. People will turn away from the sensational and will look desperately for the works of real craftsmen and artists who respect their materials. Then the works of painters like Kyffin Williams will be highly prized.[20]

Though the narrative could hardly have been more different in its particulars, it is interesting that, like Kyffin, Jack Jones was an individual who felt the need to construct for himself and present to the world an unusually detailed account of his sense of personal location, defined by family lineage and by geography. This leads me to consider another aspect of the surprisingly divisive quality of the Kyffin Williams phenomenon. The painter's intense appreciation of the visual beauty of the landscape of his home and his sensual response to it in his pictures arose naturally enough from familiarity with the places in which he spent his childhood. It developed, of course, into an intimate knowledge of the wider mountains and farmlands of Snowdonia, of Sir Fôn and Penllŷn. However, as an insider (rather than as an outsider like Turner, for instance, whose work he admired so much), Kyffin's acquaintance with the visual qualities of the land of the north-west was entangled from the beginning with a sense of the people who lived in and off that land. Here, it seems to me to be important in terms of understanding both his own attitudes and the attitudes of others towards him, to note his

---

[20] NLW Jack Raymond Jones Papers, item 14, review of Kyffin Williams exhibition at the Leicester Galleries, September–October 1966.

deep identification with a family that, if it was not particularly wealthy, was nevertheless firmly rooted in the gentry class. Kyffin Williams grew up with the values of the Anglican gentry of the high Victorian era – a group of people who, however humane he felt his churchgoing ancestors to have been, were set apart from the largely nonconformist common people and the urban middle class. Listening to recordings of Kyffin's voice, I was reminded by his clipped English accent of how many of their fundamental assumptions about the world he carried with him all his life. Among them was his generalised sense of duty, to which he sometimes attributed his basic professional motivation: 'I also feel that I must paint out of some sense of duty,' he remarked, 'but duty to what I am not quite sure.'[21] On another occasion, he speculated that it might be a duty to Wales, but I suspect that it was rather more a duty to the concept of duty itself – duty per se.

I had forgotten how hard on the ear was the spoken accent that Kyffin inherited and deployed to the end for his public pronouncements. It implied an assumption of authority and entitlement that surely alienated those who did not have the good fortune to experience the charm, marked especially by humour, that he revealed in informal situations. The same contrast was exhibited by R.S. Thomas, with whom Kyffin would become friendly in later life. Like the confidence exuded by his painting technique, and again reflecting Thomas, the tone of authority in Kyffin's voice represented in reality only half of a man simultaneously threatened by deep personal uncertainties. Nevertheless, it would be a mistake to see the one as merely a mask worn to hide the other and, therefore, to

---

[21] Meredith and Smith, p. 110. Kyffin returned to the question of duty in his autobiography, *Across the Straits* (London, 1973).

consider that uncertain self as the more fundamental reality. It seems to me that both aspects of Kyffin's character were at work together. They acted in tension, though I think that social class was particularly important not only to his sense of himself, but to the hostile art world reaction to him. The late 1950s and early 1960s produced not only abstract painting, but *Look Back in Anger* and *Saturday Night and Sunday Morning*. Kyffin could seem to some people like a relic of a discredited social order. He once remarked of his father that: 'He loved people and he could see no difference between a duke and a farm labourer', and judging from his writing there can be little doubt that Kyffin liked to think of himself in the same way – but then, it might be argued that that is what the liberally minded but socially privileged generally do like to think.[22]

In the same way that through a detailed exposition of his lineage Kyffin located himself in his writing as a person of a certain social class, the example of painters from the past was crucially important to him in locating himself professionally. He saw himself standing within the European high art tradition, as presented by the historians of his period. This is not to say that he suffered from delusions of grandeur by equating himself with the procession of 'great artists' identified in that construct of tradition. Indeed, Kyffin was always at pains to acknowledge the limitations of his achievement. Nevertheless, he did see himself as working within the security provided by an historical framework which presented visual culture as a pyramid, with the works of genius, made by the 'great artists', at the top. I mentioned earlier a visit made by Kyffin to Rome. Especially at the start of his career, he travelled on the continent to seek out the work of these artists in

---

[22] BL National Life Stories, p. 3.

the original. Those that he singled out as important to him in his later reflections upon that period of his life ranged widely, from Grünewald to Rembrandt to Rouault, but always with a distinct bias towards what we would, in retrospect, call the emotionally charged or perhaps 'expressionist' end of the spectrum. 'I love artists who would make me cry,' he told an interviewer. 'There are some Gericault is a man who would make me cry. Goya would make me cry. Rembrandt would.'[23]

However, Kyffin's understanding of art history had difficult implications for his attitude to Welsh culture. With the marginal exception of Richard Wilson, no Welsh artist figured in the understanding of European high art tradition that he absorbed, even in the English redaction of it, which optimistically elevated works by Reynolds, Gainsborough, Turner and Constable to an honoured place among the Rembrandts. Kyffin therefore accepted, apparently without question, this apparent absence of Welsh art, along with the complementary indifference of the Welsh public towards it. When, typically, he observed that: 'The people of Wales are interested in music, they're interested in literature, but they haven't got a clue about art', he was repeating a long-established trope about the culture, of course.[24] In 1907, Augustus John, one of the few Welsh artists acknowledged by Kyffin, had written of how: 'It was in truth very simple in the old days. Young artists learnt from old artists, and thus the tradition was handed down and grew. But in Wales there is no Tradition, and no really old artists.'[25] So, like Augustus John, Kyffin Williams looked elsewhere.

---

[23] Ibid., p. 94.

[24] Ibid., p. 67.

[25] Augustus John in Thomas Stephens (ed.) *Wales Today and Tomorrow* (Cardiff, 1907), p. 350.

Significantly, the received wisdom about the poverty of visual culture in Wales that Kyffin accepted was heavily promoted by the metropolitan Welsh establishment with whom he was closely associated in his early years. It included individuals (several of whom he painted) like Ralph Edwards of the Victoria & Albert Museum, who arranged for his first exhibition at Colnaghi in 1948; Dr Wyn Griffith, chair of the Welsh Committee of the Arts Council of Great Britain, on whose redaction of the *Adventures of Pryderi* Kyffin based a series of prints;[26] David Bell, who worked for Griffith as the first Art Officer of the Welsh Committee; and Sir Wynn Wheldon, who held the Chair of the Welsh Committee of the Festival of Britain, among many other London appointments. It was in the year of the Festival, 1951, that Bell wrote his picturesque first notice of the young Kyffin for the magazine *The Welsh Anvil*. However, in that same article, with all the authority of his position on the Arts Council, the author conclusively confirmed Augustus John's opinion, stating that: 'There has never been in Wales any tradition of the fine arts.'[27] Bell – 'a very nice man', as Kyffin described him later[28] – saw in the young painter's work a way out of that mythic slough of despond. In 1955 he gave him an exhibition at the Glynn Vivian Art Gallery and, two years later, wrote his notice in *The Artist in Wales*, which took the form of a eulogy extending over three pages and including two illustrations. Like Coombe Tennant, Bell had visited the house in Highgate:

---

[26] Griffith presented his stories first in a series of wireless broadcasts during the war. They were published with illustrations by Leslie Jones in 1962. It is not clear when Kyffin commenced his series of linocuts, but they were published by the Gregynog Press in 1998.

[27] *Welsh Anvil*, ed Alwyn D. Rees, vol III (July 1951), p. 17.

[28] BL National Life Stories, p. 134.

Because he paints with such energy and speed Kyffin Williams amasses a great many canvases, and his studio in Highgate was so full of pictures stacked against the wall that there was barely space for him and his easel in the centre of the room. Most of these pictures are of subjects in North Wales, but he has also painted in Pembrokeshire and in Italy [Bell added, with transparent relief] and Austria. He has painted portraits, among which is a vivid and penetrating study of Dr Wyn Griffith, the Chairman of the Welsh Committee of the Arts Council, and a Welshman in whose debt this country stands deep …'[29]

In Bell's ingratiating reference to Dr Wyn Griffith, the 'Welshman in whose debt this country stands deep', we can probably identify the immediate means of transmission to Kyffin of the 'No art in Wales' trope. In 1950, before the first of Bell's several pronouncements to the same end, Griffith had written with the certainty of profound ignorance:

So much for the past. No patron, no critic, therefore no painter, no sculptor, no Welsh art. It is as simple as that.'[30]

Given this milieu, we should not be surprised by Kyffin's negativity to the visual aspect of the culture to which, otherwise, he professed his deep allegiance. Whether we regard the disinformation purveyed by Griffith, Bell and their circle about the history of Welsh art as directly responsible for Kyffin's negativity or allow

---

[29] David Bell, *The Artist in Wales* (London, 1957), p. 170. The illustrations were the landscape *Snowdon in Winter* and the portrait of *Tom Owen*.
[30] *Welsh Anvil*, vol II (1950), p. 39.

that it may have been a confirmation of attitudes already present, it was firmly rooted by the mid-1950s. Bizarrely, he sought to turn it to advantage in the construction of his delusional image of himself as an outsider:

> I will never be an art historian as I am absorbed with my own work, but as a perpetual student of art history I make my own judgement and if any of my opinions do not coincide with those of scholars and experts, that does not worry me. Opinions, I believe, are important, even if they can be proved to be wrong. Opinion is healthy; blind acceptance of what is stated to be artistic fact is not.[31]

In due course, Kyffin's acceptance of what was, indeed, the received wisdom of the 'scholars and experts' of his acquaintance who pronounced on Welsh art, placed him in rather a paradoxical position. The English redaction of the high art tradition dominated the displays in the National Museum in the post-war period and through almost the whole of Kyffin's professional lifetime, with the consequence that the Museum found no place for the distinct interpretation of Welsh painting and sculpture. Therefore, when he became directly involved with the Museum as a member of its art advisory board, he found himself caught between conflicting inclinations. On the one hand, he had no alternative philosophy with which to challenge a high art tradition with which he himself identified but which marginalised Wales, and on the other, he was irritated by English keepers of art who were openly disdainful of the culture they were employed to present to the world. Kyffin's response was to propose the creation of a

---

[31] *Wider Sky*, p. 56.

Welsh Room at the Museum, to display the work of the small list of painters whom he saw as having contributed to the English interpretation of the European tradition – Wilson of course, and later, as his reputation grew, Thomas Jones, then Augustus John and a few others. The refusal of the Museum to create such a room depressed Kyffin. In 1974, in a letter to Jack Jones, he noted that a bout of flu – perhaps code for a *petit mal* attack – had prevented his attendance at a meeting at Cathays Park. 'It is probably a good thing,' he remarked, 'as I am certain I would have said wild provocative statements that would have done no good. I had better give it up and paint. Let the ambitious ministers and the ignorant and cowardly clots have their way ... I think I care more about Wales doing well at Rugby.'[32]

In retrospect, in 1995, Kyffin made much more of the Welsh Room argument, and presented it simply as a matter of anti-Welsh prejudice on the part of a succession of English curators, though he did so in a way that, once again, fed directly into the personal narrative of the Museum's antipathy towards his own painting:

The first keeper I brought it up with about thirty years ago, he said, 'Never as long as I am keeper will there ever be a room in the museum for Welsh art.' He was an Englishman .... Rollo Charles. And then there was a man called Cannon-Brookes who despised Welsh people entirely really, and there was no hope in him producing a room for Welsh art. Then there was a very nice man called Timothy Stevens who I got on with very well, and I brought it up at a meeting again with him and he said no, not at all, and he told a friend of mine, 'Over my dead body will there be a

---

[32] NLW Jack Raymond Jones Papers, letter to Jack Jones dated 1974.

room for Welsh art.' All these three were Englishmen. We in Wales have so few people studying art, that we cannot get a Welsh keeper, and until there's a Welsh keeper I'm afraid there will never be a room for Welsh art. I mean the Arts Committee now appointed by the new keeper, there's hardly a Welsh person on it. I am the only real Welsh person on it, and I get no support from anybody, nobody at all ... I get angry. [33]

In my correspondence with Kyffin at this time, he remarked of our separate campaigning against the policies of the National Museum that: 'You and I are both loners.' But I think that Kyffin here, as in other places, conflated being a loner with being lonely – and the two are not at all the same thing.

I believe that Kyffin's desire to establish a Welsh Room at the Museum was misguided. It would have reinforced the concept of Wales as a small contributory stream to the development of greater English culture – which, every bit as much as the outright contempt for Wales to which Kyffin rightly pointed in the persons of a succession of Keepers of Art, would have confirmed rather than undermined the 'No art in Wales' trope. However, this is not the place to pursue that argument, but rather to point out firstly how Kyffin's position on that particular matter expressed the wider British cultural context of his Welsh gentry patriotism, and secondly, that it had implications for his art. On the first point, Kyffin stood in a line of patriotic Anglocentric gentry progressives (a type exemplified in the nineteenth century by William Cornwallis-West of Ruthin Castle and in the twentieth century by Howard de Walden of Chirk), well-placed in the

---

[33] BL National Life Stories, p. 67.

English establishment, who had sought to promote the visual arts in Wales from a conviction that the people were chronically visually impaired and in need of improvement. 'What we do not have in Wales is style,' Kyffin once observed, citing as an example the Gorsedd, parading in their 'ghastly sort of nighties' as he put it, but omitting to mention that the nighties were designed by a German-born Englishman, perhaps the most distinguished artist-craftsman of the high Victorian era, Hubert Herkomer.[34] On the second point, Kyffin's convictions about the visual deficiencies of his own people cut him off from the potential offered by a different sense of artistic location that might have enriched his own imagery. I would like to explore this issue a little further with specific examples, firstly by contrasting two remarks made by Kyffin.

In 1971, in his earliest autobiographical essay, Kyffin recalled a period of his youth spent at Pentrefelin, between Porthmadog and Criccieth:

> On Moel-y-gadair I often saw the stocky, patriarchal figure of Mr Owen of Bron-y-Gadair, as he wandered, stick in hand and brindle sheepdog at his heels, to look at his flock and, I am sure, to gaze at that lovely world around him ...[35]

Here then is the affectionately recalled source of one of Kyffin's most familiar images – one that would become, for those who admire his work, emblematic of an essential Welshness. Side by side with this, consider a comment made in 1996, which exemplifies Kyffin's negativity about the visual culture of Wales:

---

[34] Ibid., p. 71.
[35] Stephens, 1971 p. 12.

The people of Wales have always appeared to me to have an unusual curiosity about their fellow men, so it is strange that we have produced so few portrait painters.[36]

Now, little more than a stone's throw from where he observed Owen, Bron-y-Gadair, Kyffin could have found in a house (that he may well have passed many times) not one but two portraits of the stocky patriarch's namesake and fellow farmer of an earlier generation, Ellis Owen of Cefn-y-Meysydd.[37] His portrait had been painted by Hugh Hughes in 1845 and by William Roos in 1850. Clearly, the very existence of these pictures of a single individual by two prolific nineteenth-century artists working in a country that had 'produced so few portrait painters' raises doubts about the reliability of Kyffin's understanding of his own culture. In fact, dozens of houses and chapels in Penllŷn and Sir Fôn were home not only to the work of these two itinerants, but also to that of the resident John Roberts of Llanystumdwy (just down the road), Hugh Jones of Beaumaris, and William Griffith of Caernarfon. Ap Caledfryn, who also grew up in the town and was first taught there by Hugh Hughes, painted a particularly striking portrait of another Caernarfonshire farmer, *Humphrey Owen of Lletty*, in 1860.

Even more revealing than simply the fact of their existence is the completely different view of the farming community that these portraits present, compared with that created by Kyffin. Roos's portrait of Ellis Owen, Cefn-y-Meysydd depicts

---

[36] *Portraits*, p. 8.
[37] The house was, in fact, Cefn-y-Meysydd Isaf. In the neighbouring Cefn-y-Meysydd Uchaf were further portraits, depicting Owen's contemporary Captain Thomas Jones and his brother, Robert, though these were not the work of Roos.

a physically impressive individual, six feet tall and with a taste for snappy dressing that expressed both his prosperity and a sense of style. He wrote poetry, including an epitaph for William Roos, and was the focal point of a literary circle that included Eben Fardd. In addition to his importance in the literary life of Llŷn and Eifionydd, Ellis Owen was active in the Anglican church and was at different times also President and Secretary of the Calvinistic Methodist Sunday Schools in the area. In the Roos portrait his hand rests on a table on which are books and a paper inscribed 'Dwyfoldeb yr Ysgrythyrau'. This image of the Caernarfonshire farmer, and others painted by Roos and Hughes, along with Ap Caledfryn's portrait of Humphrey Owen of Lletty, is utterly remote from the bent, shabby and weather-beaten stereotype created by Kyffin. The Owens of Cefn-y-Meysydd and Lletty seem to have lived on a different planet rather than just down the road from the likes of Kyffin's Owen of Bron-y-Gadair. Kyffin's images reveal the extreme level of selectivity involved in the creation of a concept that, reinforced by the early poetry of R.S. Thomas, became, nevertheless, generalised as characteristic of the nation itself, and which reinforced the perception of an archaic, melancholic, unsophisticated and residual culture. The facts are that there were many Welsh portrait painters active in the north-west of Wales in the first half of the nineteenth century, but that they served patrons found mainly among a numerous middle class who it seems did not exist in Kyffin's bipolar world of gentry and metropolitan establishment intellectuals on the one hand, and 'peasants', as R.S. Thomas would have it, on the other.[38] One must ask the question was not Kyffin's imaging of the common people, both in pictures and in words, more condescending than empathetic? Were Kyffin's anecdotes of visits to remote farmhouses, in which he described being welcomed by warm-hearted but naive natives speaking idiosyncratic English, not profoundly inflected by his very different social origins? One sometimes wonders what these people had to say amongst themselves about the painter, with his clipped English accent, after he left the kitchen.

Kyffin, the 'perpetual student of art history', appears to have been equally unmoved by a longer list of Welsh portrait painters working from the early eighteenth century down to the 1930s. Perhaps the most striking example was his older contemporary, Cedric Morris. As far as I can see, nowhere did Kyffin acknowledge Morris, surely one of the most remarkable portrait painters of his period in Britain – and one whose unsparing vision and strong colour predicts the more intense of Kyffin's own works. It is difficult to avoid the suspicion that his failure to acknowledge Morris and the others was designed to avoid diluting the impression he cultivated of his standing as the defiantly isolated loner – the myth of Kyffin's uniqueness as the truly Welsh painter.

Kyffin's adherence to the 'No art in Wales' trope extended beyond portrait painting and into landscape. Even as Augustus John was writing in 1907 about the absence of old painters from whom to learn, one of the finest ever to live in Wales was at work,

---

[38] Kyffin was aware of at least one of the portrait painters of the period, Hugh Jones. He acquired one of Jones' portraits of the comptrollers of the Anglesey Hunt, painted in the 1830s, a picture that he gave subsequently to the National Library. It is significant that this portrait was untypical of artisan practice because it resulted from gentry rather than middle-class patronage.

a few miles from where, in the company of J.D. Innes, John would soon produce his own lyrical and influential vision of Welsh mountain landscape. This was Henry Clarence Whaite. Not only as a student of art history, but also as President of the Royal Cambrian Academy, one might have expected Kyffin to have acknowledged the magnificent work of the first President of that institution. There are striking precedents in Whaite's work for Kyffin's own interest in the relationship of the farming community with the land. Like him, Whaite habitually carried a sketchbook on long walks over the mountains, recording the people and homes of the upland community and the visual impact upon their land of weather and changing seasons. Sometimes he painted finished works in the open air; on other occasions, he turned sketches into paintings in his studio on the banks of the Conwy. At a professional level there are also parallels, since Whaite, while primarily focused in his work on Wales, nevertheless became a figure of note in the London art world, in his case primarily as a member of the Royal Watercolour Society.

Just as Kyffin repeatedly presented the idea of the lonely farmer dwarfed by the mountain landscape, Whaite had returned to the image of the solitary shepherd, sometimes apparently in meditation, at others struggling to save the animals of the flock from mortal danger. The theological message of these images – the vast scale of the shrouded mountains signifying the mysterious point of contact between earth and heaven – was immediately apparent. Furthermore, just as the work of Kyffin on this universal theme has acquired a potent cultural resonance, for the contemporary critics of Clarence Whaite, the direct theological message of the pictures carried also a strong patriotic subtext. For Thomas Matthews in particular, writing in O.M. Edwards' *Cymru*, the metaphorical closeness to God of these particular landscapes implied the closeness to God also of the particular people who lived their lives in intimate relationship with them. The Welsh mountain landscape implied both a Celtic mysticism and a piety engrained in the character of the Welsh people. The former anachronistically resonated in Kyffin's attitudes till the end of his life. Not so the latter, though from the writing and interviews that he gave, it is apparent that he pondered theological issues. He suggested that while he had difficulties with elements of Christian dogma, in essence he believed in the continuity of life after death in some form, and he produced intense paintings of the Crucifixion and the Deposition.[39] Clearly, the relationship between people and land was as central to his work as it had been to that of Whaite, though precisely how Kyffin understood its implications, spiritually or culturally, was less ambiguously stated than in the case of his precursor.

Their common concern with the most fundamental issues of meaning in human life is also suggested by a focus in the work of both men on the young and the aged. In the painting *God's Acre*, Whaite's symbolism of the child supporting the old woman in the context of the ancient church of Llanrychwyn was clear. Whilst I am not aware of his having brought them together in this direct way, Kyffin chose to make many drawings of children which contrast starkly with some of his most moving imaging of those approaching death:

> I used to go to old folks' homes and paint people ... because there again was tragedy ... Most of my painting for some

---

[39] Kyffin's first Deposition was bought by Winifred Coombe Tennant for the Glynn Vivian Art Gallery. It was a subject that he repeated on two occasions. He painted two Crucifixions.

reason, it may be something to do with my epilepsy, is tied up with angst, and painting these people who are blind, or dying ... was something which appealed to this angst in me. Well, I suppose it is in me; I don't spend much time thinking all about myself but I suppose if I do think, it is this sadness which appeals to me.[40]

Clearly, then, in these portraits in particular, not only the vulnerability of the sitters becomes apparent, but that also of the painter.[41] For myself, this is the essence of their relative importance, compared with the landscapes, in Kyffin Williams' wider output. I have concentrated today on trying to understand the Kyffin phenomenon, its sources in the painter's personality and its implications *for our time* – but the portraits perhaps reveal something *time-less* about the human condition for which I suspect the work of Williams will be most valued in the future. The painter hinted on several occasions that he himself felt that the portraits were more revealing than the landscapes. In 1961 he remarked that: 'I would like to paint many more portraits as I feel I can wring more emotion from the human face ...'[42] Five years later, he acquired a studio in Bolton Gardens, by Redcliffe Road in London:

---

[40] BL National Life Stories, p. 127. Both Whaite and Williams generalised into types from individuals whom they knew personally. A perhaps significant difference between the painters was that in imaging the relationship between the individual and the mountain landscape, Whaite tended to use a young person rather than the aged representatives of the community chosen by Kyffin.

[41] Perhaps the most moving of all Kyffin Williams' portraits, that of his brother, was made with words, rather than paint. *A Wider Sky*, pp. 45–7.

[42] *Jonah Jones; John Petts; Kyffin Williams.*

Now for the first time, I had a studio in which I was able to paint portraits. I have never enjoyed working on commissions as the stress involved was considerable. Months before the sitting I began to worry, and apprehension built up as the day grew nearer; I prayed for anything to prevent the arrival of the sitter. Nevertheless I have always believed that an artist, if he claimed to be a professional, should undertake to paint anything, and so forced myself to conquer my apprehension. Once I started work, the worry seemed to slip away as my concentration grew, and I found that I was able to finish a full-length life-size portrait in a single day.[43]

These observations suggest a distinction that apparently existed in Kyffin's mind between those sitters he painted as commissions and those he painted by choice. Curiously, Kyffin maintained that 'although the money was handy' he did not accept commissions for financial reasons, but to justify himself as an artist: 'I felt, if you are asked to do something, if you didn't do it you were being a coward. I hated painting commission portraits actually, but I did it …'[44] But both in London and when he returned home, he did paint portraits for his own interest – and despite the distaste he expressed in theory for narrative painting, it would seem from his choice of sitters and the way he presented some of them in his writing, that their personal histories were as important to him as

---

[43] *A Wider Sky*, p. 211. The studio was close to the house occupied before the war by the Swansea painters Alfred Janes and Mervyn Levy, and Levy's schoolfriend, Dylan Thomas. Kyffin did not mention this though his acquaintance with John Petts, a frequent visitor there, might suggest that he knew about it.
[44] BL National Life Stories, p. 123.

their physiognomies. His record of individuals like Willy Lee, a young man from a traveller background, settled in Llangefni, are free of the stereotyping that characterised the *dramatis personae* of the landscapes.

Consistent with his peculiarly conflicted character, in his writing Kyffin sought to present an appearance of modesty by playing down any suggestion of psychological insight in these works, while simultaneously hinting at its presence. He reported that two psychiatrists had remarked on 'the way I had an uncanny ability to get to the soul of the person.' Nevertheless, it was 'something I never try to do; I mean if you paint a portrait it's difficult enough to get a likeness, and I always try and get a likeness, but to get to the soul of a subject, sitter, and to sort of psychoanalyse them is far from my mind ...'[45] That may have been so, but there exists also a level of perception beyond rational intent, as he himself obliquely acknowledged. On another occasion he remarked that 'I have simply tried to get a likeness' – but added the qualification that 'Only subconsciously may I at times have revealed some hidden aspect of the character of my sitter.'[46] When fully engaged in his work, Kyffin Williams could concentrate with remarkable intensity for periods of several hours. This level of concentration, and the exhaustion that often followed, suggest to me his ability to move to a level of perception beyond that of everyday life, in which superficialities are stripped away. The moving testimony of his friend Jack Jones tends to confirm this characteristic of the painter, from the point of view of the one painted. Jones described the powerful experience of sitting to Kyffin:

[45] Ibid., p. 54–5.
[46] *Portraits*, p. 8.

I felt very lonely sitting in the studio which was then in a sad basement. He hardly spoke at all. I felt he was struggling to make his first marks on the terrible white expanse of canvas. I did not dare speak to him. He looked at me every few seconds – moved to his canvas, made a stroke with his brush and moved back again. He squeezed his paint out of great fat tubes on to his palette and he began to attack the canvas. The studio was silent. We seemed remote, as if we were the only two people in the world. I lost all sense of time. He must have been working for hours, but there was nothing on his face that told me how the portrait was going. I felt very lonely. He wasn't painting any old object – he was painting me. I felt tired – very tired and sad. I don't know why. I think the troubles of all my days were driving through my mind. And when I saw the portrait almost finished I knew he had captured not only my head but what was in my head and in my heart. For on that particular day I was sad, and sadness was in the face he painted. The portrait was not only beautiful – it was true.

... My friends say it's not like me – it's too sad, much too sad. But they are wrong. The artist was right. He got it right the first time – spontaneously – for there seemed to be no obstacle between him and me.[47]

The sense of isolation communicated by so many of the oil portraits painted by Kyffin Williams, their pervasive loneliness, surely expresses the loneliness from which he himself suffered. It

---

[47] NLW Jack Raymond Jones Papers, item 43. Recorded for Wales TV in London 15 March 1966, as part of 'Horizons hung in air', a programme about Kyffin Williams made by John Ormond and broadcast 20 April 1966.

was the dark side of his character – the 'Williams' folly' of which he spoke to Lord and Lady Anglesey one day, when he revealed that he had been contemplating suicide.[48]

Perhaps the portraits were all, in this sense, self-portraits.

Peter Lord writes and broadcasts about the visual culture of Wales in both Welsh and English. Between 1966 and 2003, he led a project at the University of Wales Centre for Advanced Welsh and Celtic Studies which resulted in the three-volume history *The Visual Culture of Wales*. Subsequently, he was a research fellow at the Centre for Research into English Literature and Language of Wales (CREW) at Swansea University. He has curated large-scale exhibitions for the National Library of Wales and other institutions. His most recent publications include *The Meaning of Pictures* (2009), an autobiography entitled *Relations with Pictures* (2013), and *The Tradition: A New History of Welsh Art* (2016) which was chosen Creative Non-fiction Book of the Year at the Wales Book of the Year celebration in 2017. He has lived in Aberystwyth, Ceredigion since 1974, and is considered one of the foremost authorities on Welsh art and artists, both of yesterday and today.

---

[48] BL National Life Stories, p. 151.

Kyffin Williams a'r Wladfa a'i Phobl

Luned Vychan Roberts de González

Ym 1968 cyflwynodd Kyffin Williams gais i Ymddiriedolaeth Goffa Winston Churchill er mwyn, yn ei eiriau ei hun, 'ymweld â'm cydwladwyr ym Mhatagonia bell.'

Ym Mhatagonia cofnododd Kyffin bopeth a welodd – y bobl, y dirwedd, yr anifeiliaid, yr adar a'r planhigion. Wedi dychwelyd, cyflwynodd ei drysor gweladwy – yn baentiadau olew, dyfrliw, a lluniadau, ynghyd â storfa ryfeddol o ffotograffau – oll yn rhodd i'r Llyfrgell Genedlaethol ac i Gymru.

Un o'r gwragedd a'i croesawodd ac a fu'n gefn i ddilyn y Wladfa oedd Luned Vychan Roberts de González.

Yn ystod dathliadau canrif a hanner y Wladfa (1865 – 2015) gwahoddwyd Luned González i Gymru i draddodi darlith flynyddol Ymddiriedolaeth Syr Kyffin Williams.

Yn 1968, wedi cyrraedd Yr Ariannin, dechreuodd Kyffin ar ei daith yn Buenos Aires ac ar ôl iddo adael y ddinas honno mae Luned González yn adrodd hanes ei daith.

Darlith anffurfiol yw hon, peidiwch â disgwyl dim byd rhy academaidd. Dipyn bach o hel atgofion, y stori tu ôl i ambell lun, a mymryn bach o glecs i gadw'ch diddordeb. Wel lle 'nawn ni ddechrau, efallai bod rhai ohonoch chi eisoes yn gyfarwydd â chefndir y cysylltiad rhwng Kyffin Williams a Phatagonia. Ond mi ro' i grynodeb beth bynnag rhag ofn fod y pwnc yn ddieithr i chi.

Yn chwedegau'r ganrif ddiwethaf, yn 1968, teithiodd Kyffin Williams i Batagonia wedi iddo dderbyn ysgoloriaeth gan sefydliad Winston Churchill. Buddsoddiad llwyddiannus heb os nac oni bai. Bu'r ymweliad yn sbardun i Kyffin ac yn ysbrydoliaeth fawr iddo. Y mae casgliad helaeth o weithiau ganddo yn cofnodi bywyd a gwaith y gwladfawyr wedi tarddu o'r amser y bu acw yn y Wladfa. Roedd Valmai Jones Caergwrle wedi bod yn llythyru a threfnu llawer o'r ymweliad ac wedi cael addewid gan wahanol bobl y buasant yn rhoi croeso i Kyffin ar eu haelwydydd. Felly yn Buenos Aires roedd Dan Lewis, 'Dan y Bugail', yn ei ddisgwyl yn y porthladd, ac Anti Dish, ei wraig, wedi paratoi cinio croeso gan wahodd rhai ffrindia', yn eu mysg yr arlunydd Delyth Llwyd Evans de Jones yn enedigol o'r wladfa. Gwnaeth hi dipyn o argraff ar Kyffin a bu'n help iddo pan ddaeth ei baent i ben, draw yn y de. Bu arddangosfa o waith Delyth yng Nghymru ym Mhlas Glyn y Weddw.

Ni fu Kyffin yn hir yn y brifddinas gan iddo hedfan y diwrnod canlynol i Drelew. Yno, yn y maes awyr llychlyd roedd Glyn Ceiriog Hughes yn disgwyl amdano ac yn dywysydd iddo. 'A sad looking man' oedd disgrifiad Kyffin o Glyn Ceiriog mewn un erthygl. Yn ddiweddarach fe ymddiheurodd i Glyn mewn llythyr gan ddweud mai 'serious looking man' ddylai o fod wedi ei ddweud! Daethant yn gyfeillion a buont yn llythyru ar hyd y blynyddoedd.

Glyn Ceiriog Hughes

Mab hynaf Sarah Williams a John ap Hughes oedd Glyn Ceiriog, wedi ei fagu ar ffSerm Pen y Gelli yn agos at fryniau deheuol Dyffryn Camwy. Bu Glyn yn ddisgybl disglair yn yr Ysgol Ganolraddol yn y Gaiman a bu'n gweithio i Gwmni Masnachol y Camwy yn Nhrelew, yr Andes a Chomodoro Rivadavia. Yn y dref honno cafodd swydd gyda chwmni olew a gweithiodd yno tan ei ymddeoliad. Yn 1940, a Glyn bron yn hen lanc, bu farw ei dad. Cododd yr angladd o Gapel Moriah, Trelew. Yn cyfeilio yn yr oedfa angladdol roedd merch ifanc gyda gwallt coch. 'Pwy ydy'r ferch sy'n cyfeilio?' holodd Glyn, a'r ateb oedd 'May Williams, athrawes'. O dipyn i beth daethant yn ffrindie, priodi ac ymsefydlu yng Nghomodoro ble ganwyd eu plant Miriam, Diana a Ricardo. Daeth y teulu 'nôl i Drelew pan wnaeth Glyn ymddeol yn gynnar. Roedd Glyn yn ymddiddori mewn hanes ac felly bu'n ymchwilio i hanes y Wladfa, cofnodi enwau ffermydd, ysgrifennu erthyglau a hyd yn oed gweithio dipyn ar y fferm. Roedd hefyd yn gwneud llawer o waith yn dawel a di-dâl dros y cymdeithasau lleol, megis cael statws cyfreithlon iddynt, sicrhau gweithredoedd y tiroedd, archwilio'r cyfrifon, ac yn y blaen. Roedd Glyn a May yn rhyw fath o lysgenhadon i'r Wladfa ac yn fawr eu croeso bob amser.

Tra oedd o yn Nhrelew cyhoeddwyd ffotograff o Kyffin yn y papur newydd lleol, ac roedd o'n amau bod pobl wedi dychryn wrth weld y fath olwg wyllt arno yn y llun. Aeth Tegai heibio'r gwesty ble roedd o'n aros i'w wahodd i gael cyfweliad ar y radio a chofiai ei weld yn bowlio i lawr y grisiau fel rhyw wningen fawr. Bu'r cyfweliad yn Gymraeg i gyd – dipyn o her!

Euros Hughes

Nid oedd Kyffin yn hoffi Trelew o gwbl – gormod o lwch a sbwriel. ('Trelew, tre lwyd digon o faw a ddim bwyd'). Teimlai'n ddigalon efo'r lle. Felly aeth Glyn a Kyffin i nabod ardaloedd cefn gwlad Dyffryn Camwy. Aethant i gwrdd â brawd Glyn, Euros, a oedd yn ffarmwr a buon nhw'n ei weld yn dyfrio'r fferm. Roedd Glyn ac Euros yn agos iawn fel brodyr ac yn gyfeillion hefyd, yn hoffi sgwrsio am lenyddiaeth a barddoniaeth efo'i gilydd. Roedd Euros yn adroddwr penigamp, yn ŵr cymdeithasol iawn, ac yn meddu ar hiwmor direidus. Roedd o'n ffarmwr taclus hefyd, yn hoff o weld blodau a chysgod y coed poplars. Safai ei fferm ger yr afon ac roedd yn lle braf i gael picnic. Wrth gwrs, y tu ôl i bob dyn da mae gwraig dda medden nhw ac roedd Euros yn ffodus iawn yn ei briod Olwen, gwraig weithgar a ffyddlon a gadwai ardd flodau a llysiau ger y cartref, ac roedd y teulu yn ffyddlon yng Nghapel Moriah, Trelew. Aeth dwy o ferched Euros ac Olwen, Irlona a Sarah, yn nyrsys i Fuenos Aires, a Lila yr ieuengaf i fyw i Gomodoro Rivadavia. Wedi colli Euros a hithau'n mynd i oed, aeth Olwen i fyw i Buenos Aires at y merched ac yno y bu farw dros ei 90 oed. Mae gweddillion Euros ac Olwen ym mynwent Trelew. Mae'r ardd flodau yn dal i ffynnu ger eu cartref gan fod eu nith Martha yn byw yno ac yn gofalu am y lle.

Mae'n werth dweud gair am bob un o blant John ap Hughes. Fel y dywedais roedd Glyn yn cefnogi'r diwylliant Cymreig ac yn dilyn gyrfa drefol, ac Euros yn ffermio ac yn 'steddfodwr brwd. Fe sefydlodd Adah dŷ te hyfryd mewn fferm yn agos i Drelew. Aeth Gwaenydd i fyw i Buenos Aires yn genhadwr i Dystion Jehova. Roedd Thomas Hefin yn ffarmwr hefyd ac yn gweithio i gwmni'r camlesi ac yn deall cyfundrefn ddyfrhau'r Dyffryn i'r dim. Roedd Gwalia yn briod â Gwyn Humphreys a oedd hefyd yn gweithio i'r cwmni dyfrhau, hwythau'n rhieni i Martha; a'r olaf, Huw Maelor, sy'n 97 erbyn hyn yn byw yn Nhrelew ac yn Formon selog, fo a'i dylwyth. Mae amryw o'r disgynyddion yn amlwg yn y gymdeithas Gymreig.

Lle Cul a'r teulu Reynolds

Aeth Glyn â Kyffin i nabod Lle Cul, ardal a wnaeth argraff fawr arno. Un pnawn poeth clywsant lais yn siarad Cymraeg ac felly daethant o hyd i James Reynolds a'i deulu ger y bryniau serth. Roedd rhieni James Reynolds wedi dod i'r Wladfa ar long y Vesta yn 1886 ac wedi magu teulu niferus o ddeg o blant. Priododd James â Mary Roberts (un o'r 'Abergeliaid') a chawsant dri o feibion a naw o ferched. Roedd eu cartref mewn lle anghysbell ond aethai James â'r plant hynaf i'r capel tan iddo roi fyny gan fod bechgyn drwg yr ardal yn tynnu'r ceffyl o'r trap yn ystod yr oedfa. Ni chofiai ei ferch ieuengaf fynychu oedfa nac Ysgol Sul erioed. Gweithio i'r cwmni dyfrhau wnai James ac ef oedd yn gyfrifol am edrych ar ôl yr 'outlet'. O'r herwydd roedd ganddo gysylltiad ffôn yn ei gartref. Cawsai wybod pob newyddion yn gynt na neb arall yn enwedig os oedd rhywun wedi marw. Pan ddeuai galwad o'r fath, i ffwrdd â James yn ei wasgod, yn frysiog ar flaenau ei draed (fel hynny roedd yn cerdded) dan chwibanu i roi'r newydd i'r cymdogion. Roedd yn ŵr cymdeithasol iawn. Cafodd Glyn a Kyffin groeso, tot o fati, a sgwrs hamddenol yng nghysgod y coed gyda nhw.

Lias Garmon

Cymydog arall oedd Lias Garmon, sef Elias Garmon Owen. Roedd ef mewn dosbarth gwahanol gan ei fod wedi etifeddu eiddo ei ewythr Elias Owen. Roedd Elias Owen wedi gwneud arian ym Mhatagonia ac yn flaenllaw yn y gymdeithas, a gorchwyl ei nai Lias Garmon oedd edrych ar ôl busnes yr eiddo. Roedd Lias Garmon yn fonheddwr parchus, yn gwisgo'n drwsiadus iawn ac yn hynod o dda efo cyfrifon. Roedd yn gyrru modur Zodiac ar un amser ac yn byw ar fferm Coetmor. Ond nid oedd yn gweithio ar y fferm gan fod perthynas iddo, sef Dafydd Owen Coetmor yn edrych ar ei hôl. Aethai i'r dref (Gaiman a Threlew) bob dydd ac ar y ffordd yn ôl byddai'n stopio'r modur i ddosbarthu fferins i'r plant lleol. Cofiaf un tro, a ninnau wedi gwneud te i hel arian i ysgol Camwy, Lias Garmon ar ddiwedd y te yn gwneud rhodd o arian cyfartal â'r elw roeddem wedi ei wneud y pnawn hwnnw. Roedd yn ŵr cynnil ond ddim yn gybyddlyd. Efo'i chwaer roedd Lias wedi byw, bu hi farw yn 1965, ac ymhen blynyddoedd penderfynodd ymsefydlu yng Nghymru ble bu farw mewn gwth o oedran. Roedd wedi gwerthu Coetmor i Vincent, mab Dafydd Coetmor, sy'n dal i weithio'r ffarm yn llwyddiannus iawn. Roedd Kyffin wedi cymryd at Lias Garmon ac yn hoffi sgwrsio â fo. Bu Kyffin yn ei angladd yng Nghapel Garmon.

Symudodd Kyffin yn fuan i aros yn y Gaiman ac yno cwrdd ag amryw o'r trigolion, Dilys Jones, Plas y Coed, Bob Williams Aberystwyth (Bob Martha-Bob Matilda), Llywelyn Griffiths. Ni fu'n llwyddiannus yn trio tynnu llun Bob Martha ond gwnaeth lun o Llywelyn Griffiths. Mae'r llun hwnnw yn llyfr Gareth Alban Davies *Tan Tro Nesaf*. Saer coed oedd Llywelyn Griffiths ac roedd yn gwneud eirch. Bryd hynny roedd arch yn rhywbeth personol a Llywelyn Griffiths yn dod i'r cartref i fesur yr ymadawedig. Roedd hefyd yn ddiacon yng Nghapel Bethel y Gaiman ac yn arweinydd y gân yno. Mae ei fab Archie wedi bod yn ddiacon hefyd am flynyddoedd ac yn drysorydd ffyddlon i Undeb Eglwysi'r Wladfa. Yn ei nawdegau mae Archie yn awr yn gaeth i'w gartref.

Plas y Graig

Ym Mhlas y Graig y gwnaeth Kyffin aros yn y Gaiman ar y dechrau, sef cartref mam a Tegai a fi a'r teulu. Mae'n dŷ mawr wedi ei rannu'n ddau ac yn rhan Tegai a mam yr oedd Kyffin yn aros. Bryd hynny roedd mam yn wanllyd a Tegai yn gweithio yn yr amgueddfa ac roedd Kyffin yn westai hawdd iawn, yn barod i sychu'r llestri bob amser. Roeddwn i'n brysur yn yr ysgol ac efo dau hogyn bach 7 a 5 oed ac felly nes i ddim gweld llawer ar Kyffin.

Bryn Crwn

Un pnawn aeth Tegai a mam a Kyffin am dro i Fryn Crwn i gartref Ieuan ac Irma Williams. Roeddent allan ar y patio ac ar y *patch* roedd llwyth o *teru terus*, sef cornchwiglen Patagonia, yn cadw sŵn. Sylwodd Kyffin ar yr adar ac meddai, 'Mae fel tase 'na gymanfa ganu o teros'. Cafodd Irma bwl o chwerthin iach. Siwr bod Kyffin yn cofio'r Gymanfa Ganu oedd o wedi ei mynychu yng Nghapel Bryn Crwn. Mae ei ddisgrifiad o'r achlysur yn fyw iawn. Roedd yn sôn am wyneb Iorwerth Morgan ond ni wnaeth ei bortreadu, a jest *sgetsh* o Gapel Bryn Crwn sydd gennym.

Mae Capel Bryn Crwn yn dal mewn cyflwr da iawn ac oedfa yno ar Sul cyntaf ym mhob mis. Mae'r te Gŵyl y Glaniad yno yn hynod o boblogaidd, pobl yn ciwio am hir yn yr oerfel i gael mynediad a gweld y chwaraeon traddodiadol.

Symudodd Kyffin wedyn i'r Casa Británica, sef cartref Albina Jones a Virgilio Zampini. Mae Albina yn chwaer i'r ddiweddar Valmai Jones Caergwrle ac yn arlunydd medrus. Arferai roi gwersi celf yn Ysgol Camwy yn y Gaiman. Wrth sôn am *masters* y byd celf roedd Kyffin yn pwysleisio i Albina mor bwysig oedd gweld y gwaith gwreiddiol, mynychu arddangosfeydd, a ddim dibynnu yn unig ar luniau mewn llyfrau. Mae Albina wedi cyhoeddi cyfrol o hanes gwragedd y Wladfa efo llun pensil o bob un a hefyd dwy gyfrol yn olrhain achau a hanes teuluoedd y gwladfawyr. Llyfrau diddorol dros ben. Roedd Virgilio yn gyfrifol am hybu sefydlu'r amgueddfa yn y Gaiman, yn hanesydd ac athro yn y brifysgol.

Bu Virgilio yn gadeirydd Cymdeithas Camwy am flynyddoedd. Fel y dywedais, roedd Albina yn dysgu celf i blant Ysgol Camwy a chafodd Kyffin wahoddiad i draethu am hanes celf iddynt. Gwnaeth hyn yn Saesneg ac Albina yn cyfieithu a chofiaf amdano yn gwneud *diagrams* ar *sheets* o bapur gwyn yn dangos y gwahanol fudiadau celfyddydol (*movimientos artísticos / artistic movements*). Bu hefyd yn darlithio yn y brifysgol yn Nhrelew ac i gynulleidfa Edward Watkins, Byddin yr Iachawdwriaeth.

Daliai Kyffin i gwrdd â phobl y Dyffryn gydol yr amser ond doedd o ddim bob tro yn cael hwyl ar eu portreadu. Roedd Kenny Evans o Ddrofa Dulog wedi bod yn gweithio ar fferm Y Cilie yng Nghymru am gyfnod ond wrth i Kyffin geisio ei bortreadu roedd o'n chwerthin trwy'r amser ac felly roedd hi'n amhosibl gwneud darlun ohono! Roedd Barbara Llwyd Jones de Evans ar ei fferm Bron y Gân yn ardal Bryn Gwyn yn anniddig gan ei bod hi'n poeni am y tatws ar y stôf. Ond yn Lle Cul cwrddodd

Kyffin â Ceri Ellis a wnaeth apelio'n fawr ato gan ei fod yn dawel a phwyllog. Mae amryw o luniau o Ceri gan Kyffin.

Ceri Ellis

Roedd Ceri yn fab i Caroline Evans a Robert Gwaerydd Ellis (Dolwyddelan) ac wedi ei eni a'i fagu yn ardal Lle Cul. Dyn ei filltir sgwâr oedd Ceri ac yn ffarmwr gweithgar. Roedd o'n briod ag Alice Owen. Ar y dechrau roeddent yn byw mewn rhan o gartref Robert Ellis and daeth y cyfle i brynu darn o dir 40 erw yn agos at y bryniau ac enw'r fferm felly oedd Tan y Bryn. Cafodd fenthyg yr arian i brynu'r lle gan Elias Owen a gweithiodd yn ddibaid i dalu'r ddyled mewn 7 mlynedd. Symudodd y ddau i fyw yno i'w cartref newydd, gyda dim ond dwy ystafell i ddechrau. Rhaid oedd clirio'r holl dwmpathau ar y tir efo arad dwbl a gwastatáu i allu hau a dyfrio. Ni fu Ceri yn lwcus efo'r cynhaeaf cyntaf o datws felly trodd i besgi defaid. Roedd hefyd yn mynd rownd y gymdogaeth efo beindar i dorri gwenith. Rhaid oedd codi am bedwar y bore i gyrraedd cyn iddi wawrio i ddechrau'r gwaith. Roedd Ceri hefyd yn hogi sychod yn y gaeaf. Roedd yn fedrus i weithio croen anifeiliaid hefyd, gwaith sydd yn gofyn am lawer o amynedd.

Ond peidied â meddwl mai dim ond gwaith oedd bywyd Ceri. Roedd yn ŵr cerddorol, yn codi canu yng Nghapel Salem, Lle Cul, yn darllen sol-ffa yn ardderchog, ac roedd yn gallu chwarae'r *mouth organ*. Canai bâs yn y corau a'r partïon lleol hefyd. Ar ddiwedd y dydd byddai'n dal y ceffyl a'i roi yn y trap i fynychu ymarfer côr yn Bryn Gwyn ar gais Nanws Mai yr arweinydd. Deuai'n ôl yn y tywyllwch i'r cartref. Roedd hefyd yn codi canu mewn angladdau ac yn defnyddio seinfforch i gael y sŵn yn iawn. Bu Ceri ac Alice yn rhieni i bump o blant, dau fachgen a thair o ferched. Roedd Ceri yn dad reit strict ond ni fyddai byth yn codi ei lais ar y plant. Cymraeg oedd iaith y cartref wrth gwrs. Aeth Alice yn wael ac nid oedd gwellhad iddi. Y teulu oedd yn gweini arni yn y cartref yn ystod y gwaeledd.

Tan y Bryn

Un noson, a'r afon wedi codi ac yn bygwth gorlifo, roedd Ceri a'r cymdogion eraill yn 'bancio' a'r plant adre eu hunain. Cafodd Alice bwl o waedu ac roedd pawb wedi dychryn. Rhedodd y mab hynaf yr holl ffordd i Gilsat (fferm nes i fyny y dyffryn) ble roedd ei dad a'r lleill yn gweithio. Pan ddaeth Ceri adref dywedodd wrthynt 'Gall mam fynd unrhyw funud' a dyna pryd y sylweddolwyd pa mor wael oedd hi mewn gwirionedd. Roedd hyn yn 1962 a bu Alice farw yn fuan wedyn. Roedd yr hynaf o'r plant yn 16 a'r ieuengaf yn 6 oed. Cadwodd Ceri y teulu gyda'i gilydd a daliodd i fyw yn daclus a pharchus. Roedd ei chwiorydd, Anti Cathrin ac Anti Mair yn gefn mawr iddo. Pan oedd o'n ifanc roedd Ceri wedi arwyddo'r ddirwest yng nghyfnod gweinidogaeth Mr Garner a chadwodd yn driw at ei addewid gydol ei oes. Roedd y Sul yn cael ei barchu hefyd yn y cartref, pawb yn mynychu'r oedfa ac os nad oedd cwrdd yn y capel byddai Ceri yn darllen. Mae ei ddisgynyddion yn ffyddlon yn yr achos yng nghapeli Salem, Bethel a Thabernacl yn Nyffryn Camwy.

Dolavon

Bu Kyffin yn ymweld ag ardal Dolavon hefyd. Gwnaeth lun o'r stryd fawr sydd yn ochri â'r gamlas. Erbyn hyn mae'r rhan yma o'r dref yn ddeniadol iawn, y gamlas a'r coed helyg ar bob ochr iddi ac olwynion dŵr yn troi yn ddiog.

Winston Churchill Rees

Un person o'r Dyffryn Uchaf a gafodd ei bortreadu gan Kyffin oedd Winston Churchill Rees, brawd i Ivy Rees y gyrrwr bws yr oedd Kyffin wedi ei nabod ar ei deithiau 'nôl a mlaen yn yr ardal. Roedd Winston yn ffermio ger Pont Tom Bach sydd yn arwain i Dir Halen. Roedd ei dad wedi mynd i Gymru i'r Rhyfel Byd Cyntaf ac mae'n siwr bod y Winston Churchill gwreiddiol wedi gwneud argraff arno. (Cofiaf fod rhiant arall yn yr ardal wedi enwi un o'r meibion yn Lloyd George). Roedd Winston Rees yn magu da, a llygad ganddo i wybod faint oedd bob anifail yn ei bwyso, dim ond drwy edrych arno.

Arferai fynd rownd y Dyffryn Uchaf mewn trap yn gwerthu cig. Roedd o'n ddyn mawr, llond ei groen, yn hynod o gymdeithasol ac yn siarad fel pwll y môr ac yn hoffi rhannu sgwrs a glasiad efo'i gyfeillion. Ar y llaw arall, roedd ei wraig Emig yn fechan a thawel. Yn barod ei gymwynas, yn aml roedd rhywun yn mynd heibio ei gartref i ofyn benthyg arian, a Winston yn rhoi'r arian a ddim yn gwneud iddynt arwyddo'r un papur. Siaradwyd Cymraeg ar yr aelwyd ond pan aeth y plant i'r ysgol roedd y plant eraill yn chwerthin am eu pennau gan eu bod nhw'n cymysgu Cymraeg a Sbaeneg ac felly gwnaethant roi'r gorau i siarad Cymraeg yn fuan iawn. Roedd perllan yn y fferm a digon o gysgod, ac arferai'r gymuned gynnal *kermeses* yno, sef dawnsfeydd i hel arian i wahanol sefydliadau fel clybiau neu ysgolion. Roedd y nosweithiau yma'n boblogaidd iawn. Domingo Celano a Melvin Richards fyddai'n gyfrifol am y gerddoriaeth gyda'u *bandoneón* (acordion) a byddai'r llwch yn codi efo cymaint o draed yn stampio wrth ddawnsio tango, *paso doble* a *rancheras* ar lawr pridd y patio wrth olau *petromax*. Roedd cantorion yno hefyd, Elfed Evans o'r ardal ac Araneda yn dod yr holl ffordd o Borth Madryn. A sôn am Madryn cofiaf rannu taith efo Kyffin i Fadryn.

Henry ac Eifiona Roberts

Cafodd Kyffin groeso hefyd ar aelwyd William Henry ac Eifiona Roberts yn eu fferm ddim yn bell o'r Gaiman ar y ffordd i Lle Cul. Roedd Kyffin yn aml yn cychwyn allan ar ei draed efo'i daclau peintio ac yn gweithio am oriau. Bachgen amddifad oedd William Henry yn disgyn o dylwyth William Williams Mostyn. Cafodd ysgoloriaeth i fynychu'r Ysgol Ganolraddol yn y Gaiman yn 1930au ac fel Glyn Ceiriog roedd o'n ddisgybl disglair. Aeth i Comodoro Rivadavia i weithio, yr Archentwr cyntaf i gael gwaith yn y swyddfa efo cwmni o'r Iseldiroedd. Roedd y cwmni hwnnw wedi sefydlu pentref teidi i'w gweithwyr o'r enw Diadema Argentina ddim yn bell o dref Comodoro. Roedd Eifiona a'i hefaill Eirwen wedi colli eu mam pan gawsant ei geni a chafodd Eifiona ei mabwysiadu gan deulu Morgan Jones Maes Rhyddid ac Eirwen gan berthnasau o Dir Halen.

Roedd brawd Henry wedi priodi Llinos, un o ferched Maes Rhyddid, a dyna sut wnaeth Henry gwrdd ag Eifiona a dod yn gariadon a phriodi. Bu'r neithior ym Maes Rhyddid ac yno fe ddawnsiodd y Parch.Tudur Evans y *waltz* efo'r briodferch. Aeth Henry ac Eifiona i fyw i Diadema ond yn ddiweddarach dyna benderfynu dod yn ôl i Ddyffryn Camwy, gadael job dda a mentro i ddechrau ffermio ar ddarn o dir wnaeth teulu Maes Rhyddid ei roi iddynt (Cynwyl). Yn fuan sylweddolwyd bod Henry yn *allergic* i'r alffalffa a gorfu iddo chwilio am waith gwahanol. Dechreuodd drwy deithio i Comodoro yn cario nwyddau mewn lori neu *camión* ar fenthyg, yna llwyddodd i brynu un ei hun yn nes ymlaen. Cafodd ei alw i weithio i Gyngor y Gaiman a buan y cafodd ei alw hefyd i fod yn rheolwr y cwmni cydweithredol oedd yn gyfrifol am y gwasanaeth trydan yn y Gaiman gan ei fod yn ŵr gonest, gweithgar a dibynadwy.

Bu Henry yn ysgrifennydd i Gymdeithas Camwy hefyd ac roedd ar dân dros y prosiect i ailagor ysgol Camwy gan fod ei ferch hynaf mewn oedran i ddechrau'r ysgol uwchradd. Ni chredaf y buasai Ysgol Camwy wedi agor oni bai am ddyfalbarhad a brwdfrydedd Henry. Doedd dim yn ormod iddo ac roedd yn ddyn ymarferol dros ben. Pan oedd angen codi toiledau ar gyfer yr adeilad, gwnaeth Henry'r gorchwyl mewn dim o dro. Bu'n ffyddlon ac yn gefn i'r gymdeithas ar hyd y blynyddoedd. Yn yr un modd roedd yn hynod weithgar efo'r achos yn y Gaiman, gan ei fod ef ac Eifiona yn Gristionogion cadarn. Cofiaf fynd efo'r Ysgol Sul yng nghefn lori Henry ar drip glan y môr yn yr haf. Er iddo ef a'i dylwyth ymuno wedyn â'r eglwys efengylaidd yn y Gaiman roedd yn pregethu yn Gymraeg ym Methel a Tabernacl, Trelew bob mis yn ffyddlon. Mae ei fferm ar gael i'r eglwysi yn awr i gynnal gwersylloedd ac enciliadau. Mae ein cymuned yn ddyledus iawn i Henry am ei wasanaeth diflino.

Daeth yr amser i Kyffin adael Dyffryn Camwy a theithio tua'r Andes. Erbyn hyn roedd wedi dechrau teimlo'n gartrefol yn Nyffryn Camwy a dod i nabod llawer o'r trigolion, mwynhau eu cwmni a darganfod prydferthwch y lle. Cychwynnodd yn blygeiniol ar fws tua'r gorllewin a chroesi'r paith am oriau, gan drio cofnodi'r tirlun ar y ffordd a chyrraedd Esquel ddiwedd y dydd, wedi ymlâdd ac efo cur pen ofnadwy. Cafodd groeso a gwely yng nghartref Emrys a Lottie Hughes a'r bore wedyn, cododd yn y bore bach i arlunio'r oll a welsai ar ei daith y diwrnod cynt.

Tŷ Ni, Trevelin

Yn Nhrevelin cafodd Kyffin aros yn Tŷ Ni, cartref *señora* Gwenonwy Berwyn de Jones, un o ddisgynyddion yr hen wladfäwr Richard Jones Berwyn.

Nita, Norma a Paulino Quintuqueo

Pan gyrhaeddodd Kyffin i'r tŷ roedd y *señora* wedi mynd i'w fferm ar y paith ac felly cwmni Nita, Norma a Paulino gafodd Kyffin yn ystod y dyddiau cyntaf. Disgynyddion i'r brodorion oedden nhw, Nita yn edrych ar ôl y tŷ, Norma yn hogan fach ddireidus a Paulino, tua 10 oed, yn cyflawni mân orchwylion. Roedd y tri ohonynt yn siarad Cymraeg. Yn Tŷ Ni llwyddodd i gadw Norma fach yn llonydd am ychydig hefyd i gael portread ohoni, portread sydd bellach wedi dod yn boblogaidd iawn. Roedd Nita a Paulino wedi cael eu geni ar y paith. Daethant yn ifanc i Drevelin i gartref Gwenonwy, colli cysylltiad â'u cynefin a chael eu llyncu, megis, gan y diwylliant Cymreig gan eu bod yn mynychu'r Ysgol Sul a gweithgareddau'r gymuned Gymreig. Erbyn hyn mae Norma wedi symud i fyw i'r de, i Pico Truncado, ardal yr olew yng ngogledd talaith Santa Cruz, man gwyntog a llychlyd.

Yn ddiweddar yng nghartref Alwen Green holais Nita a Paulino am eu bywyd. Soniai Kyffin fod pobl y Wladfa yn *content*, bodlon, a dyna'r gair i ddisgrifio agwedd Nita a Paulino. Mae Nita wedi magu teulu ac yn dal yn gryf ei ffydd Gristionogol. Mae Paulino hefyd yn gadarn ei ffydd, yn gweithio i'r dalaith a chanddo ddwy ferch yn *profesoras*, sef athrawesau ysgolion uwchradd. Cofia Paulino'r diwrnod pan aethant i'w nôl i fynd i Drevelin gyntaf; dengyd a chuddio trwy'r dydd yn y creigiau tan y cafwyd hyd iddo a'i gyrchu i Drevelin. Ni fu erioed yn ôl yn ei ardal enedigol.

Cwm Hyfryd

A dyma Kyffin bellach yng Nghwm Hyfryd, rhan o'r wlad oedd yn gwbl wahanol i Ddyffryn Camwy. Roedd mynydd Gorsedd y Cwmwl yn codi yn urddasol, coed a chysgod ym mhob man. Cafodd Kyffin fenthyg ceffyl at ei wasanaeth iddo allu crwydro'r ardal. Roedd Kyffin yn dotio at y marchogion lleol a gwnaeth aml i lun ohonynt ac o olygfeydd Cwm Hyfryd.

Brychan Evans

Cafodd Kyffin gyfle i ymweld â chartref Brychan Evans, patriarch y lle, a oedd yn byw mewn fferm ddim yn bell o bentref Trevelin a gwnaeth bortread ohono. Roedd Brychan yn fab i Esther Williams a Dalar Evans ac wedi ei eni yn Nyffryn Camwy yn 1882. Ymfudodd y teulu i Gwm Hyfryd yn 1894 ac ymgartrefu yn Nhroed yr Orsedd, lle y mae Eluned Morgan yn sôn amdano yn ei llyfr, *Dringo'r Andes*. Roedd Brychan yn ymfalchïo yn y ffaith ei fod o wedi teithio rhwng yr Andes a Dyffryn Camwy ar ei draed (pan oedd o'n gwneud y *servicio militar* – gwasanaeth milwrol, gorfodol bryd hynny), ar geffyl, mewn wagen, mewn modur a hyd yn oed mewn awyren. Roedd yn farchog penigamp ac wedi dringo llawer o fynyddoedd Cwm Hyfryd ac yn gallu defnyddio'r *lazo* (lasŵ) a'r *boleadoras* (peli hela) yn ardderchog.

Priododd Brychan â Mary Thomas, merch Elizabeth a Rhys Thomas yn 1915, mynd o gartref Mary i'r Ynadfa ar fferm Underwood a gorfod cerdded rhan o'r ffordd yn ôl i gartref Elizabeth a Rhys Thomas.

Y bore wedyn, adroddai eu hwyres Nora wrthyf, daeth cnoc ar y drws yn gynnar iawn, Elizabeth oedd yno; "Codwch blant! Mary, mae'n rhaid i chi fynd i odro. Brychan, mae angen codi tatws." Yn fuan penderfynodd rhieni Mary fynd yn ôl i fyw i

Ddyffryn Camwy i ardal Treorky a gadael y tŷ, y dodrefn, y fferm a'r offer i'r pâr ifanc. Roedd Mary yn wraig weithgar, a'r un modd Brychan. Roedden nhw'n cadw gwartheg, fo yn godro a *separetio* a hithau'n gwneud menyn. Bu Brychan yn gwerthu llaeth a menyn yn Nhrevelin am ryw ugain mlynedd ac ar ôl hynny gwerthu'r llaeth a'r menyn o'r fferm. Arbenigodd ar fagu da Shorthorn.

Roeddent yn aelodau yng Nghapel Bethel, Cwm Hyfryd, a Brychan yn ddiacon. Arferai ddarllen ei Feibl adref a dewis yr emynau i'r oedfa ac roedd yn arwain parti plant. Roedd ganddynt gartref lletygar a chroesawus iawn, gyda pherthnasau, cyfeillion ac ymwelwyr yn galw heibio'n aml ac yn aros yno. Pan oedd rhywun yn nesu at y tŷ, allan â Mary a Brychan bob amser i roi croeso cynnes a'u gwahodd i mewn. Roedd teisen bob amser ar y bwrdd te, yn ogystal â'r bara menyn a'r jam wrth gwrs. Roedd ganddynt gar ac yn barod i gario pobl ynddo bob amser. Gwyddai Brychan hanes cynnar y Cymry yng Nghwm Hyfryd ac roedd yn fawr ei barch yn y gymuned. Bu farw yn 1971 bron yn 90 oed. Roedd Mary wedi ei ragflaenu dair blynedd ynghynt.

Tierra del Fuego

Cyn gadael y wlad teithiodd Kyffin i Ushuaia yn Tierra del Fuego yn y de a hefyd ymwelodd â thref Bariloche yn nhalaith Rio Negro, ardaloedd sy'n denu llawer o dwristiaid.

Pan gyrhaeddodd Kyffin yn ei ôl i Lundain, doedd dim sôn am ei offer peintio na'r bocs arbennig yr oedd saer y Gaiman wedi ei baratoi iddo i gario ei holl waith. Wedi chwilio'n fanwl daethpwyd o hyd iddynt yng nghrombil yr awyren. Diolch am hynny yntê! Meddyliwch gymaint tlotach fuasem ni i gyd hebddynt. A chymaint o bleser mae cynifer o bobl wedi ei gael o nabod y Wladfa trwy ei lygad artist o.

Ond hoffwn bwysleisio bod Kyffin wedi ysgrifennu llawer hefyd am y Wladfa. Mae ei atgofion yn llawn hiwmor ond yn hiwmor sydd ddim yn brifo. Oedd, roedd o'n ŵr bonheddig. Trosglwyddodd ddarluniau gan artistiaid o Gymru i Ysgol Camwy gan roi mewn grym beth oedd o'n ei gredu ac yn ei bregethu, sef ei bod hi'n bwysig gweld y gwaith gwreiddiol.

Byddai amlen a cherdyn Nadolig efo'i lawysgrifen nodweddiadol yn cyrraedd yn brydlon bob blwyddyn. Arferwn anfon llythyr neu gerdyn ato, a'r tro diwethaf anfonais un mi ddaeth nodyn yn ôl i ddiolch wedi ei ysgrifennu gan ei nyrs.

Yn 1998, i ddathlu pen-blwydd Kyffin yn 80, bu arddangosfa o'i waith yn amgueddfa'r Gaiman. Cafwyd eu benthyca gan wahanol bobl oedd wedi cael y lluniau yn bresant gan Kyffin. Yn yr agoriad roedd amryw o'r rhai roddodd lety i Kyffin yn bresennol ac roedd y sgwrs yn llawn atgofion amdano.

Do, mi fu penderfyniad Cronfa Winston Churchill i roi ysgoloriaeth i Kyffin yn un doeth iawn. Diolch yn fawr am hynny.

Precis: Kyffin Williams a'r Wladfa a'i Phobl

Based on those people painted by Sir Kyffin during his historical four-month visit to Patagonia in 1968-69, this essay by Luned Roberts de González is a brilliant, moving, warm, and personal look at the people of 'Y Wladfa', her compatriots, as featured in the book *Gwladfa Kyffin/Kyffin in Patagonia*.

As part of the fabric of the community in the Gaiman, Luned Roberts de González is in a unique position to animate Kyffin's portraits with her detailed and pertinent observations regarding the men, women, and children she knew and knows so well. Dress style, family lineage, social history, contributions to society, occupations, makes of cars owned by those active in society – it's all here in this fascinating essay by the Samuel Pepys of Patagonia – Luned Roberts de González.

∽

Ganed **Luned Vychan Roberts de González** ym Mhatagonia yn 1936 - yr ieuengaf o blant Arthur Roberts a Mair ap Iwan, Plas y Graig, y Gaiman. Mae'n byw yno hyd heddiw.

Mae hi'n or-wyres ar ochr ei mam i Lewis Jones a Michael D. Jones, dau o sefydlwyr y Wladfa. Hefyd, mae'n or-nith i Eluned Morgan, un o brif awduron y Wladfa, oedd yn rhannu'r cartref gyda'i nith a'i theulu.

Fe'i haddysgwyd yn yr ysgol gynradd ac yn yr Ysgol Ganolraddol yn y Gaiman, lle cai'r Gymraeg, y Saesneg a'r Sbaeneg oll eu lle. Fe'i haddysgwyd wedi hynny yn Nhrelew cyn mynd i Buenos Aires i gymhwyso fel athrawes Saesneg.

Dychwelodd i'w hen gartref lle magodd hi a'i gŵr, Virgilio González o Buenos Aires, ddau fab, gan rannu'u cartref gyda'i chwaer, Tegai Roberts.

Caewyd yr Ysgol Ganolraddol – sef Coleg Camwy heddiw – yn y pumdegau, ond ym 1963 mi ailagorodd, gyda Luned González yn brifathrawes arni hyd ei hymddeoliad yn 2002.

Yn ystod y cyfnod hwn bu cryn ddeffroad yn y diddordeb yn yr iaith Gymraeg a'i diwylliant ac roedd cyfraniad Luned yn gwbl allweddol i'r cyfan.

Ei chwaer, Tegai Roberts, ddechreuodd y rhaglen radio wythnosol sy'n cadw'r gymdeithas Gymreig ynghyd, ond ers ei marw daeth Luned yn gyfrifol amdani. Hi, hefyd, fu'n cydlynu'r Prosiect Dysgu Cymraeg ac yn gofalu am yr athrawon a deithiai o Gymru i'r Wladfa.

Mewn cydnabyddiaeth o'i llafur diflino dros y blynyddoedd, fe'i hanrhydeddwyd gan OBE, ac fe'i derbyniwyd yn aelod o Orsedd y Beirdd yng Nghymru ac o Orsedd Beirdd y Wladfa.

Kyffin Williams & R. S. Thomas – Attitudes to Wales and to Faith

Dr Barry Morgan

Some of you here tonight will probably be thinking that to speak about a poet and an artist in the same lecture is a bit like comparing apples to oranges, especially from somebody who cannot claim to be either an artist or poet. Now, I know that bishops of past generations were great patrons of the arts and indeed employed both poets and artists, but I am afraid those days are long gone – Ichabod, the glory has departed. And as I said when I opened the summer exhibition at the Royal Cambrian Academy one year, when Kyffin was its president, I never ever got more than 20% for my artwork in school, and to the relief of my teachers, gave it up in my second year at grammar school. The only comment I

ever got was, 'Will never be any good but tries his best'. So I am
no artist and have never tried to write poetry.

So then, why speak about an artist and poet? Well, both
were famous Welshmen, one born in Llangefni and the other in
Cardiff; both had an enormous affinity and love for Wales, its
landscape and history, especially north Wales; they both lived
at different times in Chirk, on the Llŷn peninsula, Meirionnydd
and Anglesey, and they were born within a few years of one
another – R. S. Thomas in 1913 and Kyffin in 1918. Both lived
into their eighties. R.S. was 87 when he died in 2000, and Kyffin
was 88 when he died in 2006. They of course knew one another,
but apparently did not talk about either poetry or art – just about
rugby and birds! Both lived frugal lives without benefit of much
comfort. Kyffin's home in Pwllfanogl could hardly be described as
luxurious, and R. S. lived most of his life without fridge or TV; the
electric cleaner was never used because it was too noisy, and he
ripped out the central heating in Rhiw for the same reason. More
personally, they were people whom I admired from a distance as
I grew up in a mining village in south Wales. I never thought that
I would ever meet them, or if at least I did, that I would not get to
know them, but I was privileged to do both as Bishop of Bangor,
and I officiated at both their funerals. Both wanted simple ones.
R.S. got one, in the small Pentrefelin church at the end of the lane
in which he lived. There was no music, no hymns and no homily
on his instructions. Kyffin would have preferred a simple service
at Llanfair-yng-Nghornwy, but the burial there was preceded by a
service at Bangor Cathedral. I had to persuade him that a service
of that nature was required.

Kyffin sketched a portrait of R.S. after the latter's retirement.
'Look at it,' said R.S. to me once. 'It makes me look very

miserable'. I am afraid I gave him little consolation when I said that at times he did appear to be so. All I got by way of a reply was 'Humph'. Ironically, R.S. Thomas was married for the second time in Llanfair-yng-Nghornwy, where Kyffin is buried. Kyffin's great grandfather had been the rector there. As I think of them both, I am reminded of a moment in R.S. Thomas's *The Echoes Return Slowly* in which he asks, of himself, had he ever been anything but solitary, and of Kyffin's admission that when he was at Trearddur Bay School and Shrewsbury, he was always a loner. Nicholas Sinclair, Kyffin's godson, has said that Kyffin told him there was a mood that touched the seam of melancholy that is in most Welshmen, a melancholy derived from the dark hills and heavy clouds and enveloping sea mists. 'Melancholic' might well have been a description for R.S. as well. Writing poetry and painting are solitary occupations, and one thinks of R.S. spending every morning writing poetry and of Kyffin either in his studio or out walking the mountains, sketching and painting. Both were great nature lovers, and R.S. spent his afternoons walking and birdwatching and gaining inspiration for his poetry. Both R.S. and Kyffin give the lie to the attack once made on Wales by A. N. Wilson in the *London Evening Standard* when he said, 'The Welsh are held in universal derision. They have never made any significant contribution to any branch of knowledge or culture. Choral singing, usually flat, seems to be their only artistic attainment. They have no architecture, no gastronomic tradition, and since the Middle Ages, no literature worthy of the name. Even their religion, Calvinistic Methodism, is boring'. It simply shows up Wilson's ignorance, for here were two giants in their respective fields.

On Poetry and Art:

R.S., of course, was no stranger to art. Mildred Eldridge, his first wife (he called her Elsi), was a very talented painter and a Fellow of the Royal Watercolour Society, and had been to the Royal College of Art. I have one of her paintings. Elsi's artistry was something that drew R.S. to her; he identified with the artistic life she led and yearned to prove himself in his own field. She was a well-known artist long before he became a well-known poet. Eldridge's great mural, *The Dance of Life*, painted for the orthopaedic hospital in Gobowen, has now been loaned to the University of Glyndŵr in Wrexham. It consists of six panels painted in oil on canvas, telling the story of humanity's alienation from nature and the attempt to reclaim a lost, natural wisdom. It has images of plants, animals, birds, the countryside and the sea.

His wife's attention to detail when rendering birds and plants helped R.S. in his observation of the natural world. Quite simply, she helped him to look at things. He referred to some of his wife's paintings in his *Selected Prose* (1983) on chapels such as Maes yr Onnen and Soar y Mynydd but, ironically, did not possess any of her paintings after her death. She produced more than 2,000 finished pictures, in oil and watercolour, and regularly exhibited at the Medici and Beaux art galleries in London, and her work as an artist for Athena Cards helped finance the household. Her son credits her with resurrecting the art of fine-detail natural history studies. She also illustrated children's books, as well as being a sculptor.

R.S. wrote a number of stirring poems about paintings, following other poets such as Seamus Heaney, Dave Smith, Derek Mahon, W. H. Auden, Euros Bowen, Christine James, Tony Conran, and Gillian Clarke, but as Professor M. Wynn

Thomas has pointed out in lecture, R.S. 'was participating (no doubt unaware and most uncharacteristically) in a popular, even fashionable, modern trend of writing poems about paintings'.

In his volume entitled *Between Here and Now*, R.S. wrote poems about 33 Impressionist paintings chosen from a book by Germaine Bazin, *Impressionist Paintings in the Louvre*. These contain landscapes, seascapes and portraits of various kinds, but almost half of them have women as their subject. R.S. found the Impressionists in particular useful in focusing his response to women. He referenced artists such as Monet, Degas and Renoir. Wynn Thomas has argued that those poems in which R.S. explores womanhood in an intense way are a natural extension of what R.S. had done since he began composing, in that his poems had always contained strong, graphic images and painterly qualities.

The number of painting poems R.S. wrote, in comparison with the number he wrote about farmers or God, are relatively few, and thus are often underappreciated. According to his own writing, R.S. viewed art as many things – a leisure time activity, but also something sacred and spiritual that reveals something profound about human existence. But, as Wynn Thomas points out, what is being addressed in a poem about a painting is a representation of a representation – the art of art. And of course, just as one can read into a poem several layers of meaning which were perhaps not intended by the poet, so too is it possible to look at a work of art and see things the artist may not ever have intended. Thus, in the poem 'Portrait of a Young Woman', R.S. ignores Degas' intentions, and chooses to see the sweetness and youthfulness of the subject's character rather than just her physicality. The poem imagines how this young girl might arouse sexual feelings in the on-looker, but implies that she herself is somehow waiting to be aroused as well. There is scarcely a poem in which R.S. addresses a female subject wherein he is not also sexually troubled in some way. Writing on Tolouse Lautrec's *Jane Avril Dancing*, R.S. notices the dancer's tempting knees; in Mary Cassat's *Young Woman Sewing*, he writes of the red flowers surrounding the subject, hinting at the inevitable arrival of her period.

Of course, I do not know what Kyffin Williams' feelings were as he drew and painted women, but I do not get an impression of repressed sexuality. Kyffin, although unmarried, was totally at ease in the company of women, and some of the women he knew were utterly devoted to him. During his last illness, he would never have gone hungry, as casserole after casserole was brought to him. Ironically, R.S. too was very comfortable in the presence of women and enjoyed their company. If R.S. interpreted great art in his own way, he himself did not mind people reading his poems in whichever way they wanted. After one such reading at the University Church in Cambridge, he had supper with Peter Walker, then the Bishop of Ely. The bishop asked R.S. to tell him the meaning of a few lines of a poem. 'It is as it reads,' R.S. answered. The bishop protested that the poem could mean a whole host of things, depending upon one's perspective and interpretation. 'The poem is the poem,' R.S. persisted. 'So there is no explanation, then?' the no doubt somewhat frustrated bishop asked. 'Certainly not from me,' said R.S.

In 1955, a number of Welsh artists paid visual tribute to Thomas' poetry by producing paintings based on a selection of his poems. The paintings were displayed at Oriel Glas y Weddw, and reproduced in a book entitled, bilingually, *Ysbrydoliaeth R.S. Thomas Inspiration*. Contributors included David Tress, Donald

McIntyre, Tony Goble, William Selwyn, Gwilym Prichard, and Peter Prendergast – and of course, each interpreted their chosen verse in their own particular ways, some in quite abstract form. Kyffin, of course, never claimed to be a poet, but he did write limericks. I am not sure what R.S. thought of them. Kyffin illustrated some of his limericks and regarded the book in which they were collected as a bit of light relief and lunacy. He admitted that it wasn't really the done thing for artists to illustrate such comic verse, but viewed it as his own sort of rebellion against a snobbery that he felt pervaded the art world. Kyffin claimed that he liked poetry, but that reading it gave him a headache.

On Family:

There is no doubt that R.S. had a rather difficult relationship with his mother, for he wrote about it often enough. He never quite forgave her for not teaching him to speak Welsh, and found her overbearing and dominant. He often referred to his mother's presence as being rather negative, and his prose and poems are peppered with references to her possessiveness. In his autobiography, he recounts the agonising story of leaving for university and experiencing his mother's desperate sense of loss. His father, a merchant seaman, was for him a loving but distant figure, to whom he often refers with longing. His father, who was often absent at sea or, later, nearly inaccessible due to deafness, aroused in R.S. a longing for place, particularly for Wales and Welshness. R.S. tells a story of how, when he was a young boy living near the sea in Liverpool, his father once directed his attention to the mountains far away to the west. 'That's Wales,' he was told.

Kyffin too believed that he had inherited from his grandfather, via his mother, a certain neurosis that was responsible for the melancholy and loneliness that often pervaded his landscapes. Kyffin's mother would not speak Welsh, though his father loved it. Kyffin, like R.S., preferred his father, from whom he learnt sociability and affability. Kyffin's father, a bank manager, loved people. When Kyffin's grandfather, a priest, baptised him, it was done in English – only the second time, apparently, that he had used English in his entire ministerial career; the first time had been when he baptised Kyffin's elder brother, Dick. Kyffin's mother banned the use of Welsh in the house, something Kyffin referred to in later years as brainwashing, for it meant that if anyone outside the house spoke Welsh to him, he would 'switch off' involuntarily. Yet he himself spoke the language fluently and used it extensively. In fact, Vaughan Hughes, in an article he wrote for *Barn*, said that Kyffin would not have been able to gain the trust and co-operation of the monoglot farmers immortalised in his paintings without his knowledge of Welsh.

R.S., of course, came to the language later, but learnt to speak it fluently. He wrote his autobiography in Welsh, but bitterly regretted that he could not write poetry in the same language; he did not regard his Welsh-language prose as a substitute. Kyffin recited poetry in Welsh and titled most of his paintings in Welsh – in fact, as has been pointed out by David Meredith in his volumes on Kyffin, he claimed that he painted in Welsh.

But just as in R.S.'s case with his own mother, it wasn't just the fact that Kyffin's mother forbade him to speak in Welsh that made for a difficult relationship. He believed his mother had little time for him, and much preferred his brother Dick. His mother had sent him to a wet nurse for the first year of his life, a farmer's wife in Llanfechell. Kyffin described his mother as a very affectionate person by nature who nevertheless did not feel it appropriate to express affection, and so he grew up without it; he was sad for himself, but also for her. R.S.' mother, on the other hand, smothered him with affection and love until he felt suffocated by the weight of it. Much as Kyffin, hurt by his mother, sought to understand her, R.S. too came to feel later in life that he had judged his mother too harshly.

On Profession:

Kyffin became an artist almost by accident; he had always wanted to join the army. At Shrewsbury, from 1931-36, he played the bugle in a military band and went with the Officers' Training Corps to a camp in Wiltshire. He joined the 6th Battalion of Welsh Fusiliers. Because of his epilepsy, however, he was invalided out of the army, much to his regret. It was the army doctor, in fact, who encouraged Kyffin to take up art, since he was 'so abnormal already'. R.S., by contrast, was never much enamoured with the military. When he became the vicar at Eglwys Fach, he was appalled to discover that there were quite a few retired army officers living there who were not at all used to having a nationalist, pacifist poet as their parish priest. But as Kyffin became an artist because of his epilepsy, R.S. also followed an unusual route to ordination. His anglicised Anglican mother, who had grown up in her brother's clerical household, encouraged him in his calling as a priest – a calling R.S. himself admitted was a bit unorthodox since, at the time, he didn't attend church regularly. It was rather that he had no strong objection to the idea of being a candidate for Holy Orders, and so was open to his mother's encouragement. God calls people in mysterious ways, R.S. wryly concluded.

But just as Kyffin had hated his boarding school at Shrewsbury, so R.S. hated St Michael's Theological College, Llandaff. Kyffin had been unable to make friends at Shrewsbury and, because of his smallness, could not participate in rugby. Some of his teachers regarded him as stupid. He hated the puerile traditions of the school, the elimination of any vestige of a regional accent, accompanied by beatings if not successful. Meanwhile at St Michael's, R.S. yearned for the familiar life and backdrop of the North. There were no open grounds at St Michael's; no mountains, no place to walk except along the main road. Worse still, the year was divided into four terms, which meant that he had to return to school in the middle of summer. Whatever peace R.S. may have found in his calling as a working priest, neither the routine of college or the college itself ever appealed to him.

On God and Religion:

Many of Kyffin's forebears, on both sides of his family, were Anglican clergy. His grandfather, Owen Lloyd Williams, was Canon Chancellor of Bangor Cathedral and Rector of Llanrhuddlad, and married the daughter of the rector of Llanystumdwy. Kyffin's uncle, his father's brother, was rector of Coedana in Anglesey. His mother was the daughter of the rector of Llansadwrn – the whole family was involved in some way or another in the religious life of Anglesey. Yet Kyffin himself often mentioned that he was not a believer, although he did enjoy singing in the Shrewsbury School chapel choir on Sundays for the sense of security and respite the atmosphere there gave him. He also enjoyed being dressed in his white surplice and rich, red cassock, and felt at ease in that ornate place of worship.

Kyffin never considered himself religious, and indeed associated the word 'worship' primarily with the adoration of women, but claimed that the experience of exploring the mountains of north Wales gave him a greater sense of emotional and even religious feeling than all the confirmation classes of his school days. To him, God's beauty was all around, to be seen freely and not interpreted with what he saw as prejudice. There are echoes here of R.S. Thomas, who said that God revealed Himself to him more through the beauty of the natural world than through people. His poem 'The Moor' likens being in those open spaces to being in church. Kyffin's faith, in spite of his disclaimers, seems to have been straightforward and simple, whereas R.S. Thomas's was an anguished one – so much so that some have accused of him of being an atheist. He was far from that, but, whilst believing in God, he did not avoid any of the hard questions that such belief entails. He always said it was not the being of God he questioned, but the nature of God in a world full of cruelty and chance. There was also the question of God's seeming absence or hiddenness – questions with which many mystics had also struggled. Like many others, R.S. had difficulty with prayer; he saw it more as a waiting, listening, and receiving from God rather than a demanding of things from Him, as if one were presenting God with a shopping list of requests. It is obvious he spent hours in church seeking a relationship with God, and was sometimes rewarded, which seemed enough for him. As R.S. said himself, 'If there was no God, there would be no possibility of finding Him.'

Kyffin did not usually paint religious subjects himself, but he has said that the first painting to make a real impact on him, to show him what art was all about, was *The Resurrection* by Piero della Francesca. He also counted the religious works of Botticelli, Crivelli, and Rembrandt among his influences. Above the fireplace in his living room hung an ornate carving by Jonah

Jones on Llanberis slate of a quotation from Psalm 4, in Welsh: *Fel y brefa yr hydd am yr afonydd dyfroedd felly yr hiraeth fy enaid amdanat ti* (As the hart longeth after the water brook, so longeth my soul after thee, O God). He would not have had such a verse in his living room had faith not played some part in his life. It was the late Bishop Ramsey who said that sometimes it is simply enough to want God.

R.S., of course, in spite of his tortuous relationship with God, and in spite of the fact that he felt it was impossible to understand God fully, nevertheless felt that without God, his being was empty. He returns to this idea again and again in his poetry, and to the quest for God – and for this reason, is regarded by many as the finest religious poet of the twentieth century.

On Authority:

R.S. Thomas was not comfortable in the presence of gentry, the military, or people who hunted, although his son, Gwydion, claims that he aspired to be a country gentleman. Kyffin was very relaxed in the company of such people. Both men in their different ways were, however, anti-establishment. Kyffin fought long and hard against the art establishment and had some pretty harsh things to say about it. He felt that the general stance of the art community against anything one might call 'tradition' was short-sighted, the product of evil-minded people who believed 'tradition' was holding back the future of art. But to Kyffin, that tradition was an outward expression of humanity; to reject that art was to reject an aspect of humanity. He derided art exhibitions at the Mostyn Art Gallery in Llandudno which consisted of two flickering television monitors in a large empty room showing similar scenes of inane objects performing inane acts, empty of meaning. He also despaired of the deteriorating standards at the annual Arts & Crafts Exhibition of the Eisteddfod. Kyffin was angry when the Wales Art Advisory Committee of the National Museum, on which he sat, turned down his advice for purchasing a painting by Gwen John because they felt she was of little worth, and he had clashes in the 1970s and 1980s with the Welsh Arts Council and with Peter Jones, its director. He eventually resigned from the board of management of the Mostyn Art Gallery. The clashes had consequences. When he was asked to be an art judge at the National Eisteddfod in Cardigan, it was only for the children's competition; an artist from abroad was brought in to judge the main work. Dr Mike Stephen's obituary for Kyffin, years later, highlighted the fact that he had been neglected by the Welsh Arts Council for many years.

R.S. Thomas too clashed with those in authority. Throughout his time as a priest in the Bangor diocese, Gwilym Williams was bishop and later archbishop. Here was an archbishop with a First in English and a First in Theology who had this brilliant poet in his diocese, and the two simply did not get on. When R.S. retired at the age of 65, he offered to look after his former parish of Aberdaron, without a stipend, whilst continuing to live in the vicarage. The bishop refused, even though R.S. need not have retired until he was 70. At Bangor, I came across a record of a diocesan court which Bishop Gwilym had asked his chancellor to hold. R.S. had apparently not received a certificate of banns from a young man, on the morning of his wedding, showing they had been called, as was required by law, in both Aberdaron and the man's church. R.S. had ascertained from the groom's friends, however, that the banns had indeed been called in the man's parish and so had gone ahead with the wedding. It was not enough for the bishop, who got his chancellor to come from Essex, and a court was held in the churchyard at Aberdaron one Saturday morning. R.S. was chastised for not having got the certificate of banns, but since he had gone to the trouble of discovering that they had been called, he received only a mild rebuke from the chancellor. I expect the bishop had decided to invoke such a procedure because R.S. probably flouted Episcopal authority in all kinds of ways. He once said, 'I always thought there was something wrong with a chap's head if he wanted to become a Bishop'. (I think, however, the episode shows how pastorally caring R.S. could be. He could have refused to marry the man concerned but did not. It is worth remembering that, because he has been accused of being uncaring towards his parishioners). I remember the first time I met him, when I was the Archdeacon of Meirionnydd and went to sympathise with him on the death of his first wife. He told me that he had spent his life avoiding people like me, but then invited me in to have tea with him. He had never been asked to read his poetry in any church in Wales and I persuaded him, or rather his second wife persuaded him, to read it at Bangor Cathedral when I was bishop. She told me afterwards that the reception I gave after it, at the bishop's house, had been a kind of healing experience. He felt, as it were, that he had been acknowledged and accepted. Rumour has it that R.S. burned his cassock after retirement. He did, however, continue to attend church regularly.

On Landscape:

There is no doubt that Kyffin and R.S. were passionate about the landscape of north Wales, and it was this landscape, both confessed, which fired their imaginations. The places which inspired Kyffin's work were the cliffs of South Stack in Anglesey, where R.S. had spent his boyhood; and Eifionydd and the Llŷn, where Kyffin had spent part of his childhood and where R.S. spent the latter part of his ministry. Kyffin, however, said that the real foundation of his art began when he lived in Pentrefelin between Cardigan Bay and Cwm Pennant, with Moel y Gadair in front of his house and Llŷn to the west. It was also the village to which R.S. finally retired. Kyffin, of course, was born in Anglesey and spent the latter part of his life at Pwllfanogl where he could view the Eryri range. He said that he often visited South Stack to watch the sea birds and wonder at the primeval conclusions that created the distorted bands of rock. He found the geology of Anglesey even more fascinating than its natural history. Kyffin plastered oil thickly on canvasses, giving his paintings depth and engendering a feeling of awe. He was what Tony Jones called in his lecture 'an emotional and gutsy artist – aggressive, expressionistic, handling of thick piles of paint to make a surface that is churning, restless and dynamic'. R.S. too, of course, was a great birdwatcher and was interested in geology. Birds in particular, he admitted, gave him more pleasure than human company, and he compares waiting for birds to come with waiting for God to reveal Himself to him. But as Kyffin told David Meredith in a 2003 programme for Fflic Productions, what he loved to paint were 'the mountains and the sea, the sun on the hills and the heavy dark clouds, the sun breaking through them and the sea bright and the moon red among the clouds'. As Tony Jones put it in his own lecture, 'Kyffin found the heart and soul of Snowdonia, the most ancient DNA of the Welsh landscape, and he put it in the paint'. For R.S., the countryside was indispensable to his faith. He wrote in his autobiography that glimpsing a bit of blue sky through bare tree limbs was the same to him as looking at a stained-glass window in a cathedral. The descriptions of Welsh landscape in his poetry sometimes resemble Wordsworth in their imagery. Neither he nor Kyffin, however, were sentimental about nature. One only has to look at some of the dark mountain scenes of Kyffin and the roughness of some of his seascapes to realise he knew all about the force of nature. R.S.'s prose and poetry, as well, turned at times to contemplate the mercilessness of nature. Nature, beautiful as it was, was also red in tooth and claw, and humans could be crueller than any animal. It was recognition of this violence and suffering that caused R.S. to ask questions about God's part in it – for either there was another force at work, thwarting God's will, or God was somehow responsible for it. It is a question philosophers and theologians have asked from time immemorial.

On People:
Kyffin said of himself that he cared deeply for people – he was, in his own words, 'obsessed with them'. He was at home with them and, as I have said already, had he not had an affinity with the locals, they would never have allowed him to portray them. He seemed always amazed that people in Wales liked his art and were prepared to buy it, and was genuinely humbled by that fact.

It was often said of R.S. that he did not like people. His hawk-like face and wintry smile gave the impression of aloofness and remoteness. He could be offhand and pretend not to understand English when tourists asked for directions in Aberdaron. He was known as the 'Ogre of Wales', and some of his poems even seem to hold farmers in disdain, calling them irreverent 'docking mongrels' who were rarely mirthful. He spoke of them as being tough and materialistic, measuring one another by the acre or the pound; men who turned their back on their culture and gone into trade in Welshpool, Oswestry and Shrewsbury.

Yet, when one looks at Kyffin's portraits of farmers closely, I am not sure how flattering they are. The overcoats have been used for a long time, and they are usually tied with string; the caps are a bit skew-whiff and the figures look a bit vacant. Perhaps, like R.S., he was depicting what he saw, and I am not sure that anyone took offence at Kyffin's portraits. R.S. says that in his poems, he is speaking for farmers and describing how they might feel, but his poetry about people and about God express all his feelings as well, and show a kind of love/hate relationship with both. There is a total honesty in describing what he actually saw and felt.

Both R.S. and Kyffin, of course, depict farmers battling against the elements where the winters are raw and figures bend as they push against the winds, working hard to earn a living. R.S. said that the farmers probably never read his poetry and I suspect that, in the end, most farmers depicted by Kyffin would not have been able to afford to buy pictures by him. The author Nigel Williams, when describing Kyffin's work, talked about people who 'look with all their eyes' and make sense of what they see for others. The same sentiment could apply to R.S. That is what these poems and portraits do.

Jackie Davies, I discovered after writing this lecture, wrote a dissertation on both men for a fine arts degree in 2004, and she suggests that both men use pared-down language in their art. Kyffin used a minimal palette of colours, and R.S. was economic in his choice of words, yet at times overflows with love – a love that, according to his son, he was unable to express in his relationships. There was, he says, no double bed in the house, and he does not recall ever witnessing his parents touch one another, but there could be no doubt about R.S.'s love for his wife – it was there in the poetry he wrote for her. It is worth remembering that R.S. was much loved by most of his parishioners in Aberdaron (none of us can be loved by everyone) and was always there in their hour of need, in spite of the fact that he had no time for small talk. Even in his less-flattering poems about farmers, there is a tenderness, even a love, which must be considered alongside his harder strictures. R.S. could be vitriolic in his views about his fellow Welshmen, whom he felt had kowtowed to the English and allowed them to take over parts of Wales to earn money. Kyffin seems to have felt none of that vehemence.

On Obsession:

Both of these men were prolific in their output, almost obsessive; Kyffin was drawing during his last illness, and R.S. worried about not being able to write poetry in his old age. Kyffin himself said that obsession of that sort was important – that having a talent meant you could do something easily, but that to have an obsession meant you were driven to do it. It's a word that is attached to them both over and over – David Meredith's biography of Kyffin was called *Obsessed*, and Wynn Thomas's latest book on R.S. Thomas is entitled *Serial Obsessive*. In R.S.'s case, his obsession was theme: Wales, God, and love. The creative acts of any artist, he felt, were the echo of God's original creative impulse. Echoing Coleridge in his introduction to the *Penguin Book of Religious Verse*, R.S. says that the nearest we approach to God is as creative beings. Great art brings both creator and observer closer to the primary imagination – and, in a way, nearer to the actual being of God. This is surely why, then, that both of these great artists, in their different way, appeal to so many people, and why Wales is so very proud of them.

Dr Barry Morgan served as Archbishop of Wales for fourteen years, between May 2003 and January 2017, when he retired from the post on his 70th birthday. Before retirement, he was the longest-serving archbishop in the worldwide Anglican Communion. Originally from the small mining village of Gwaun-Cae-Gurwen in the Swansea valley, Dr Morgan attended the universities of both London and Cambridge before being ordained in 1973. During his ministry, he served as a university and theological college lecturer and university chaplain, and as Rector of Wrexham and Archdeacon of Meirionnydd before being consecrated as Bishop of Bangor in 1993 and Bishop of Llandaff in 1999. He also served on the Central Committee of the World Council of Churches and on the Primates' Standing Committee of the Anglican Communion. Dr Morgan has served as Pro Chancellor of the University of Wales, and is a Fellow of the Learned Society, as well as several Welsh universities. He has a long-abiding love of the poetry of R.S. Thomas; his book on the subject, *Strangely Orthodox: R.S. Thomas and His Poetry of Faith,* was published by Gomer in 2006.

Images and Meaning

Dr Rowan Williams

It is a great honour and privilege for me to accept the invitation to deliver this Kyffin Williams Memorial Lecture, and I am taking the opportunity to indulge myself in a subject not so much about theology, but about some of those aspects of art which I believe, in the long run, open some crucially important doors in the direction of theological discourse.

I want to begin with what may seem a very basic question: what is a painting doing? Is a painting there to remind us of what things look like? A kind of keepsake, a souvenir of transient experiences? Any practising artist will, I think, say without hestitation that it is something else. It is not a souvenir or a keepsake; it is not a reproduction of or substitution for the world around us, nor even an imitation of it. The word that is most often in my own mind to answer this question is 'representation'. It's an important word not just for thinking about paintings, but also for thinking about what human beings are fundamentally like – because I do not believe there is much point in talking about art unless, in the same breath, we are prepared to also talk about its role in making us human.

A very familiar phenomenon in the history of art is the propensity of the visual artist to return again and again to the same subject: refiguring a landscape, re-imagining a face, re-examining a collection of objects. If art were simply fixing one's own set of perceptions on canvas, there would be no particular need to go back again and again to a subject – and yet, think of Rembrandt's repeated self-portraits. Rembrandt never finished looking at his own face, it seems. Think of so many of the great French Impressionists, recreating haystacks and water lilies. Think of van Gogh and his sunflowers. Welsh artists are not immune to this. One of my favourite examples is Gwen John – a great artist, and underrated by many. Not only does she portray repeatedly the very typical nineteenth century theme of a chair in an empty room, but she also left an extraordinary series of paintings of Mother Marie Poussepin which she began and never completed. Marie Poussepin was a French nun, founder of the Dominican Sisters of Charity of the Presentation; Gwen John was asked to provide a series of paintings of the founder of the order, one for each room in the convent. The result is a sequence of paintings of one woman's aging face framed by a nun's wimple, all of them as radically and challengingly different as any other set of paintings that John completed. What is it that compels artists to return in this way and re-visit what looks like the same thing? Part of the answer is surely that, for Rembrandt or Seurat or Manet or even Gwen John, the return is an attempt to see what it is that lives in a face or a landscape or an object – what it is that lives beyond any one moment. And that, I think, is somewhere near the heart of what a painting seeks to attain and to represent. What is it at the heart of what is seen that has shape and energy that is not exhausted by any one encounter with it?

All kinds of art tell us, I believe, that what we encounter in our environment is not exhausted by the encountering. with 'Hopkins' famous poem 'God's Grandeur' represents one way of capturing that sense of relating to things that we never come to the end of. Just as it would be rather eccentric if someone said, 'I think I've now heard enough performances of *The Magic Flute*,' so the artist in encountering the environment says, 'I will never have looked my last on this scene, this face, this object because I am encountering something that is not exhausted in any one moment.' Each individual encounter is at the centre of unique circumstances, a sameness of diversity.

That seems to me to be the key to understanding how artists – particularly visual artists like the ones I've mentioned – approach their work, and it helps us perhaps understand why they focus upon what might appear to be quite narrow fields. However, to speak of Kyffin Williams's field as 'narrow' is in many ways misleading. He is not by any means a local or regional artist – or at least, he is not only those things; and yet, we do observe in his work a constant and obsessive return to repertoire of subjects, scenes, and even faces that is the very opposite of stale or repetitive. A similar observation could be made of Josef Herman – another Welsh artist, though not Welsh-born. Do we call Herman's revisiting of the faces and scenes of Ystradgynlais in the 1940s and 1950s a 'narrow focus'? I hope not. It is merely that the apparent limitation of subject matter is due to a sense, on the part of the artist, of never having come to the end of even what is most familiar. It is not always necessary to go far afield for inspiration because what is familiar is also what is most strange, and most inviting. No doubt that's why Rembrandt, who presumably knew his own face fairly well by old age, still wanted to paint it – because he did not yet understand himself, any more than he understood anybody. And the artist celebrates that moment of joyful not-understanding.

I hope this explanation helps to cast some light on my opening point – that the act of representation is something different from reproduction or imitation, from the work of a formula or diagram. If we talk about reproduction or imitation, we talk about something that is essentially rather static. We say this feature corresponds to this feature, and that one to that – we map one onto another. Lewis Carroll once not entirely jokingly remarked that the ideal map is one that is exactly the same size as its territory – but of course, perfect correspondence is not what maps are for. And as to formulas and diagrams, the American art critic Nelson Goodman pointed out some decades ago that the data found there is necessary for a clearly defined purpose. In a mathematical formula, you may add a small curlicue to a number or a symbol; you may even, if you like, draw some leaves twirling around the side of a triangle. But the part of the formula that matters is not the details you have added – it is the essential shape, corresponding to the particular cluster of information required.

But artistic representation is very different. You don't know quite what is necessary and what is not. You're not dealing with a clear set of data directed toward an equally clear set of purposes.

You might look at a formula decorated with illuminated numerals or twined leaves and decide that the decorative elements don't matter, but it would be a very rash person indeed who, pointing at a canvas, said, 'Well, that square inch doesn't matter.' The work has a life as a whole, and you cannot separate out what is intrinsic, or contingent, or accidental.

As it happens, Mr Goodman does not like the word 'representation' any more than he likes 'imitation', when applied to art. He does not feel either is helpful. Sometimes the terms 'representational' and 'non-representational' are used to differentiate between art that looks like something else and art that doesn't. Goodman points out that this misunderstands what is going on in a painting – discussing representation as if it were an idiosyncratic physical process like mirroring. Representing isn't mirroring; representing is seeking how to make one piece of the material world transparent to one particular set of perceptions. If art is therefore not reproduction, not substitution, not imitation, and not entirely representation – perhaps we may use the word 'continuation'? Instead of correspondence or representation, we should talk about the continuity between what is seen or felt and the artwork which embodies those things in another way.

So it seems we are thinking about the work of art as an object which seeks to be transparent or open to the activity of something that isn't. It looks to allow the form, the life, the energy sensed by the artist to live in another vehicle, another medium. The French Catholic philosopher and critic Jacques Maritain talked about the pulsions, or rhythms – the clenching and unclenching, the light and the dark, the tight and the slack, the pulse and alternations of the world. Although he applied it mostly to the work of poetry rather than visual art, one can see some continuities there, I think.

So what is going on in a painting? Certainly, in a sequence of paintings around the same subject, there is an attempt to allow to emerge some unity of action or event which the artist's activity is trying to align itself with. Which brings me to another word I find helpful here: alignment. The artist is not seeking to get out there what happens to be going on in an individual subjectivity. Equally, the artist is not just trying to reproduce what he or she is seeing. The artist will be looking, listening, and feeling for the pulsions – that unifying energy, the active logic of what is being observed. How do I represent that rhythm, that movement? So you won't be surprised to hear me say that there is a properly contemplative dimension to art as there is to prayer. You're trying to be aligned, you're looking and listening so intently that it could be painful, and what emerges as your work of art emerges from that intensity of looking, listening, and feeling. And that's maybe why the best portraits, in my opinion, aren't painted from photographs. They are painted from that time-consuming process of looking at another face in a different light, with those subtly, illusively different shadows and contours that emerge moment by moment. Often the best thing one can say about a portrait is not that it looks so much like its subject, but that it gives a sense of life, that there is a potential change in every line.

I should perhaps declare a sort of personal interest here, in that my sister-in-law, Celia Paul, is a fairly well-known painter who has, for most of her career, focused on painting about five people. Of the work she has produced in the last thirty years, I would say some 85% has been restricted to her mother and her sisters. And one of the things to which she is positively allergic is painting from photographs – she could not, I think, conceive of the operation I have just been describing as emerging from looking at a photograph. That relation of observation, of moment and almost imperceptible shifts in light, expression and contour is part of the essence of what's going on here. We might quite reasonably say that the artist seeking to be aligned with what is going on is seeking to be, in the very literal sense, informed so that the artist may perform what is there. What is a painting doing? It's performing. That sounds a very strange phrase, I daresay, but I believe very strongly that that is what is going on in a good painting: it's performing, it's allowing a form of activity to be there in a new way, and thus of course it informs and is performed by the viewer not as an object to be passed by, but as something which makes subtle difference over a long period of time to the observing self.

Aligning, informing, performing. And the truthfulness of a work of art, painting or whatever, is therefore not a matter of checking off correspondences A, B, and C. It's, to borrow a word from Nelson Goodman once again, a matter of aptness. Is this apt, is this fitting, is this, to use a good Welsh word, *addas*, in relation to what is there? If one were to meet Rembrandt face-to-face, standing next to one of his self-portraits, I think one would say that it is apt, that it is fitting – not so much that it looks like him, but that it's an appropriate, continuous presentation of what's there. The initial data that the artist works with becomes almost like a musical score – it's there to be performed. The artist brings it alive in a new medium, just as the score on the paper is rendered alive in the voice's or instrument's delivery of it. Which is why a work which is apparently a good, competent reproduction of a particular scene may have no real aptness or truth to it, and why a work which may, at first sight, seem very unlike anything you have ever seen, may be truthful and apt in a quite different way. And yet so much of the culture we've inherited in the western world, certainly up until the twentieth century, has assumed that truthfulness or realism mean correspondence in a rather narrow way. Quite a few years ago, the great Sri Lankan writer on aesthetics, Ananda Coomaraswamy, wrote of the strange situation of showing a tribal chief in the Pacific Islands a portrait which a missionary had drawn of him. The chief, finding he did not recognise the image at all, produced in reply a representation of the pattern of the tattoos on his face. The reproduction of what his face happened to look like was neither here nor there for him. Coomaraswamy took this as a ground for broadening our definitions of realism and truthfulness in art. I remember viewing the images he describes in my twenties, and seeing very vividly what he meant.

I could digress here into thinking about and reflecting on that powerful tradition, especially in eastern Christian religious art, of the icon, which does not seek to reproduce or resemble, but seeks very explicitly to capture an energy, so that what matters in the religious icon is not whether an image looks like St Basil, but whether, in encountering it, praying with it, energy that is St Basil is transmitted to the viewer. Now that carries with it a complex set of theological theories which again would take a long time to elaborate, but it's not a million miles away from what I think any serious artist would have to say – 'I'm not trying to show you what it's like, you can do that for yourself; I'm not trying to give you a souvenir or a postcard. I'm trying to allow a life to live, to be performed, to communicate.' Which doesn't mean that artistic representation can never be life-like, but that life-likeness in our usual sense means quite a lot of expansion, quite a lot of opening up to these deeper levels of continuity and informing. To be like the life of what we see is never going to be a matter of the photographic souvenir.

Now coded in all this, I think, is a set of insights about the way the world actually is, and what kind of world we as human beings inhabit. We are quite used to thinking of the self as, in the words of one twentieth century philosopher, rather like a lighthouse circulating its beam on a lot of passive objects. To know something is to fix it in that beam for a moment and, as it were, to photograph it, to capture it. But what if the world around us is in fact constantly seeking to be known, so alive that its life overflows, demanding response – alignment, information, performance? Part of what the artist, in particular the visual artist, seeks to do, I believe, is to say that what is seen is a metaphor – but an important one, offering itself to be seen, requiring to be explored, inviting us not as observers but as sharers in something. And I believe quite strongly that what we see in the work of an artist that we deeply value is the representation of a world which invites, which says 'Go on looking' – because the more you look, the more alive you are as an observer. The life that is present in a work of art is transmitted in such a way that you become more alive in looking at it. That is to say, your own rhythms and patterns of understanding, of imagining, are deepened and extended in the encounter with this object.

So the final work expresses, as I've said, neither a set of data nor a state of mind; instead, it's the fruit of a process of attending to an active form. The face, the object, the landscape represented is not yet fully itself until it has lived in you as the observer. Which means, of course, that our relation to our environment is a great deal more implicated, a great deal more involved, and much less distancing and controlling than we might sometimes think. One of the paradoxes of the intellectual history of the last century or so is that, on the one hand, popular and half-understood ideas about scientific process have reinforced for so many the idea that 'out here' there is a lot of passive stuff, and 'in here' is an active mind interpreting it all. The active mind organises the passive stuff into tidy bundles, labels it and stacks it, and that's science. And yet in the last century or so, the further reaches of scientific enquiry have made it more and more clear that that is conspicuously *not* how science works – that the observer's role in observation changes what is being observed, and the observer is, in fact, participating in the process they are seeking to describe. Curious as it may seem, the world of the creative artist and the world of the creative scientist are far closer than a lot of our educational philosophy would allow them to be. The more conscious we are of that, I think, the healthier and more exciting our intellectual life, as a culture, will be.

Michelangelo was not the only sculptor to say that, when he embarked on hacking away at a piece of marble, he was seeking to liberate something that was already there. Although that's a particularly powerful image in the context of the sculptor, I would guess it's not completely alien from what a great many visual artists in other modes seek to do: they are seeking to let what is there be free in a new medium, to transcend one set of limitations and enter into another shape. You could say that's a fundamental aspect of our consciousness itself, that we are always allowing one form in diverse embodiments and realities to shape our mental processes. We can't think without analogies about making connections, analogies about sameness or indifference.

And so to answer again my question, what is a painting doing? It is reminding us what we're doing when we think. In a sense, when we look at a painting, we realise that what the artist has done is what we are constantly doing ourselves – absorbing, organising, re-presenting, receiving a life, configuring it in some way in our minds, letting it live in a new mode. It's all so profoundly part of what we actually do when we think that it is hardly surprising that visual representation has been part of the life of homo sapiens as far back as we can go. Some of you may have seen the exhibition of Ice Age art last year in London. Some twenty thousand years or so before the Christian era, we can see artists in the caves of central Europe representing the life around them – presenting the reindeer in the haft of a knife, its swimming form on the curve of the ivory handle. Sensing a movement, a shape, a form, and having this extraordinary intuition that that shape, that form, that mode of action can be caught again in a completely different mode. The sense is there that life can live somewhere else, and it's been there, in our human response to the world we're in, for as far back as we can know.

But I want to touch on one other aspect of all this which I think is quite significant in a world where we often forget it: art takes time. I believe that serious visual art always declares something about the time it's taken. I don't mean that one looks at a great painting and says, 'That must have taken a few weeks to do'; I mean that the very material shape of a painting may tell you something about the time it's taken to create. You don't exhaust what's there with a single glance; you realise that what's gone into the making of a work of art is the passage of time. Quite often, with many great artists, you'll see this expressed in the corrections, the visible re-workings of a surface. You'll see it in some of Kyffin's paintings, of course: in the intense use of the palette knife, where the surface of a canvas can become quite ridged and mobile because of the action of the knife which constantly sculpts and re-works what's there. You'll see it as well in the later work of Rembrandt, the sense that again and again a surface has been re-thought, re-worked because the alignment has not yet fully come into focus. And to me, that is one of the most moving things about the greatest of paintings – the sense of time taken. Whether or not expressed in these particular, physical ways, what is there is something a great deal more than a snapshot or souvenir. The famous statement attributed to both Eliot and Auden that a poem is 'never finished, only abandoned' fits aptly here. I think that has a lot to do with why, in looking at a Rembrandt self-portrait, at some of Kyffin's self-portraits, we see what people sometimes call a face that's been inhabited, a face that someone has grown into – because the portrait itself somehow embodies the time it took to get to look like that.

So I believe that good painting, in addition to reminding us how we think, also reminds us that we live in time – that we are not simply the particular set of operations working in this instant; we carry with us all the time that has made us, and that the selfhood we are now is something which the past has shaped and that the future will continue to enact upon. This is also why a good painting requires us to view it from more than one angle. There is no ideal point from which to look at a painting. You move around, you look at it in different lights, from different angles, and discover different things. You walk around and put together all these wildly diverse angles and points of view and, very gradually, something much more than any one of them comes into your mind, is performed for you.

The same is certainly true of sculpture. I remember looking at a set of sculptures in the garden of the Bishop's Palace in Exeter some fifteen years ago, where there are three large, monumental statues supposed to represent the Holy Trinity. Now painting pictures of the Holy Trinity, let alone creating sculptures, is a dangerous and rather eccentric occupation. What struck me about these particular figures was the simple fact that you couldn't see them all at once from any one point of view. There was no way of taking in that cluster except by weaving in and out of them and putting together in your mind those multiple perspectives. You had to take time. On a smaller scale, you will see this in any gallery – people looking at painting from one angle and then another, from one distance and then another distance, recognising that what they are seeing is not something to get to the bottom of in one go.

But how, to address the broad theme that I've been hinting at throughout, does all of this relate to what we are as human beings? I think, in all that I have said thus far, what is emerging is a picture of our humanity which challenges a number of attractive cultural myths. I said, for example, that it challenges the idea that our knowing is always the result of focusing a beam of light from in here to out there – from the active self to the passive world. In that sense, it also challenges the exploitative and instrumentalising approach to the world we're in which has been so much of the curse of particularly Western and north Atlantic civilisations for the last couple of centuries, the consequences of which we now live with in the form of environmental crisis. To understand how and why art works as it does is to understand why this model of thinking won't do, if we really want a human future. It won't do to sit down passively with that idea of the relation of active human and passive world. It also, I think, challenges some of those fictions which, in the post-modern era, are still very attractive: namely, that it is possible somehow to cut ourselves off from the time that has made us who and what we are, that it is possible to, as we often say, re-invent ourselves. Many aspects of our culture encourage us to think that we can in some sense regard our own identities, our own possibilities, as so many consumerist objects – some to be retained, some developed, others discarded. The practice of painting in the way I've described it is a practice which recalls to us that we are time-bound, as well as bound in matter and space. We are where we are, and reminding us of that deceptively simple fact is something else that a painting does.

That's why, to come clean theologically at last, I think there's something spiritual about a great work of art. Not in the object itself – but in the working of it. Spiritual not because it points to eternal values or transcendent realities of mysterious depths of creativity – it no doubt does all of that – but because I would argue that the most authentically spiritual thing that can happen to us is for us to be reconnected with the life in the middle of which we are living. And the most anti-spiritual thing we can experience is a life which isolates us from the place and time in which we find ourselves, from the world in which we are in. It's been one of the greatest and most popular mistakes in talking about the spiritual: to suppose that it is essentially about escape. But this is where I very much like the old Zen Buddhist remark that before you begin meditation, mountains are mountains, rivers are rivers, and trees are trees; when you start meditating, mountains and rivers and trees cease to be mountains and rivers and trees; and finally, when you obtain enlightenment, mountains, rivers, and trees are what they are again. Or, as T.S. Eliot puts it in his *Four Quartets*, the end of our exploring is to arrive where we started and know the place for the first time. That is the spiritual – certainly in a tradition like our own, which values essentially the notion of incarnation, that the transcendent is present in the very depths of what is most familiar and most real.

The work of painting, like all sorts of other arts, declares that inexhaustible depth and that inviting quality in reality around us. It says that what you see is something you will never come to the end of. The spiritual work that belongs to art is the work of constantly opening up in ourselves that space where we realise that perhaps our growth and our horizons are without limit. Not in the sense of being released from the specific, the local, but because there is no end, in principle, to what can be thought, seen, unfolded in our experience of the environment in which we stand. And of course, it is true indeed that we stand in the middle of interlocking systems of action, forms of active life, moving in upon us, inviting us to share them. That, to say the least, connects with the theological idea that the most fundamental form of life is sharing, bestowing or giving. Of course, not every visual artist or viewer of art wants to be committed to a theological world view, but as a theologian, I find it at the very least encouraging – the sense of inexhaustibility, the sense of listening for and aligning to intelligent action. That at least fits with the kind of universe that I, as a religious believer, take seriously. But whatever one makes of that, we come back to a sense of what a painting is doing: it is showing us who we are. A mirror is not the most helpful of analogies, but art certainly prods us into self-recognition. What is a painting doing? It is telling us what we're doing when we think, and also witnessing a humanity engaged with the world it's in, seeking restlessly and constantly for a more apt, a more continuous, and so more truthful relationship with what is given to it.

Dr Rowan Williams served as Archbishop of Canterbury from 2002 to 2012, and as Archbishop of Wales from 2000 to 2002 – he preceded Dr Barry Morgan in the post. Born in Swansea to a Welsh-speaking family, Dr Williams left Wales to study theology at Cambridge, Oxford, and College of the Resurrection in West Yorkshire. He was awarded the degree of Doctor of Divinity from Oxford in 1989, and an honorary DCL degree in 2005, as well as a further honorary DD from Cambridge in 2006. He is a Fellow of the British Academy, the Royal Society of Literature, and the Learned Society of Wales. Dr Williams is a noted poet and translator of poetry; aside from Welsh and English, he speaks or reads in eight other languages. Currently he is serving as the Master of Magdalene College in Cambridge, where he resides with his wife Jane.

O Fôn i Fenis
David Meredith

Yn y flwyddyn 1950, gwelodd John Kyffin Williams ddinas ryfeddol Fenis am y tro cyntaf.

Gŵr yn ei dridegau oedd Kyffin pan groesodd y Sianel am y tro cyntaf, yn drwmlwythog gyda'i offer arlunio, ar ei ffordd i ddinas Rufain i ddechrau, cyn mynd oddi yno i Fenis. Canlyniad i'w epilepsi oedd y daith gyfandirol hon gan i awdurdodau'r sefydliad meddygol yng Nghanolbarth Lloegr awgrymu na ddylai weithredu fel athro am flwyddyn ac y dylai gael gwyliau mewn awyrgylch gwahanol, dan amgylchiadau gwahanol. Dyma sut y bu iddo fynd ar daith i Roma a Venezia.

Yn ninas y camlesi, cofnoda Kyffin iddo gael lle i aros mewn hostel ieuenctid gyda chroesdoriad rhyfeddol o ddynoliaeth: Ffrancwyr, Iwgoslafiaid, gŵr o'r Affrig a âi i'w wely gyda chyllell sylweddol wedi'i chlymu wrth ei byjamas, hanesydd celf o Guatemala, nifer o Americaniaid, Sais swnllyd nosweithiol feddw a gwynai dan gablu am y *ffyg* yn y stafell wely; cwmni amrywiol yn wir — cwmni perffaith ar gyfer gallu disgrifiadol Kyffin.

Cofnoda Kyffin hefyd ei fod wedi bod yn hapus yn Fenis, ac er ei bod hi'n anodd iddo, oherwydd ei epilepsi, weld yn iawn yn yr awyr agored yn yr haul llachar, cafodd wledd weladwy o weld gwaith y meistri yn yr eglwysi a'r galerïau. Ys y dywedodd Kyffin, "Deuthum dan gyfaredd gwaith celf Fenis".

Rhaid cofio, erbyn 1950, fod Kyffin wedi bod yng Ngholeg Celf y Slade, coleg oedd wedi symud o Lundain i Rydychen adeg y rhyfel ac wedi bod yn athro celf hŷn yn Ysgol Highgate, Llundain am ymron i ddeng mlynedd ar hugain. Yn y coleg daeth yn arbenigwr ar hanes celf.

Bu Kyffin yn hynod ffodus o astudio dan yr Athro Carl Tancred Borenius o'r Ffindir, Athro Hanes Celf cyntaf Coleg Prifysgol Llundain. Roedd yr Athro Borenius yn awdur toreithiog ac yn un a gydnabyddwyd fel un o'r arbenigwyr byd ar arlunio Eidalaidd cyfnod cynnar y Dadeni Dysg. Roedd ei lyfr cyntaf yn seiliedig ar ei waith ar gyfer ei ddoethuriaeth, sef astudiaeth o beintwyr Vinzenca, nid nepell o Fenis.

Roedd Borenius nid yn unig yn athrylith, ond yn gymeriad lliwgar hefyd. Credir iddo weithredu fel ysbïwr ar ran Prydain yn ystod yr Ail Ryfel Byd, tra'n gweithredu fel diplomat i'r Ffindir — y dyn yma oedd Gamaliel Kyffin ym maes hanes celf. Taniwyd Kyffin gan Borenius ac ymhyfrydodd mewn hanes celf, ac felly doedd enwau Tiziano Vecellio (Titian), Jacopo Robusti Tintoretto, Giorgione, Francesco Guardi, Giovanni Bellini, Canaletto a Veronese, rhai o brif arlunwyr Fenis ddim yn enwau dieithr iddo.

Gwyddai am eu harbenigedd unigol, gwyddai mai mewn olew yn bennaf y gweithiodd Titian gyda'i bortreadau meistrolgar. Gwyddai'n ogystal am fanylrwydd peintiadau Canaletto a luniai beintiadau *veduta* (h.y. golygfa) gyda chymorth *camera obscura*, lluniau manwl a chywir o'r hyn a welai. Edmygai wychder peintiadau Francesco Guardi a ddechreuodd yn peintio veduta ond a ddatblygodd arddull fwy rhydd — lluniau wedi eu peintio gan symud y brwsh paent yn gyflym. Bychan yw'r peintiadau o bobol ym mheintiadau Guardi. Ni phoenai ormod am fanylrwydd pan beintiai ddynoliaeth yn ei beintiadau o weithgarwch morwyr ar lannau'r Gamlas Fawr er engraifft, a bu'n destun syndod i lawer sut y gallai sblotsyn o baent, o edrych arno'n fanwl, gynrychioli dim mwy na sblotsyn o baent, ond wrth ymbellhau oddi wrtho, hynny ydi sefyll yn ôl, ymddangosai'r sbotyn paent fel ffigwr dynol —tric a champ yr arlunydd.

Guardi oedd ffefryn Kyffin. Iddo ef Guardi yn hytrach na Canaletto cyflwynodd wir deimlad o Fenis. Dywedodd Kyffin pan fyddai'r awyr yn Fenis yn troi'n ddu-las a phalasau'r Gamlas Fawr â gwawr lliw arian arnynt, yna byddent yn ymddangos fel ym mheintiadau Guardi - arlunydd oedd yn sensitif i'r tirlun a'r awyrgylch arbennig a berthynai i wahanol leoliadau.

Yn 1975, blwyddyn dathlu 'Treftadaeth Ewrop', penodwyd Kyffin yn Gadeirydd 'Pwyllgor Dathlu Treftadaeth Ewrop' — un o bwyllgorau Cymdeithas y Celfyddydau yng Ngogledd Cymru.

Bryd hynny wrth ysgrifennu cyflwyniad i lyfr ar Michaelangelo dywedodd y pensaer Dewi Prys Thomas, "Digwyddodd y Parthenon yn Athen bedair canrif cyn Crist oblegid dau reswm holl-bwysig, agosrwydd marmor Mynydd Pendelicon a dyfodiad y meistr Sifias. Yn yr Eidal wele fynyddoedd y Carrara — mynyddoedd y marmor perffaith yn aros canrifoedd am y dyn â'r cŷn — y dyn hwnnw oedd Michelangelo". Ac mi ddywedodd Kyffin rywbeth tebyg iawn am Fenis. Wrth esbonio sut y daeth yr arferiad o beintio mewn olew o'r Iseldiroedd i Fenis tua 1474, pwysleisiodd Kyffin yr elfen o lwc a fu yn hanes datblygiad celf. Yr oedd Fenis y cyfnod, a ddaeth yn ganolfan i rai o arlunwyr mawr y byd, yn ddinas forwrol rymus, rymus iawn ac yn yr iardiau llongau roedd aceri lawer o ganfas, h.y. hwyliau'r llongau — perffaith ar gyfer peintiadau olew. Lle cynt y ceid peintiadau *tempera*, peintiadau ar bren yn defnyddio gwynnwy yn gymysg â lliwiau — peintio ar raddfa cymharol gyfyng — heddiw, gan ddefnyddio olew ar ganfas, gellid peintio peintiadau ar raddfa llawer mwy gyda symudiadau brwsh mwy mentrus, mwy eofn. Mi fentra' i ddweud "heb ganfas heb hwyliau llongau Fenis, dim Canaletto, dim Guardi", wel dim fel yr ydym ni'n adnabod eu gwaith nhw heddiw!

Fel y dangosodd Dewi Prys Thomas, mae'n rhaid cael y deunydd crai sylfaenol a phwrpasol cyn y gall unigolion creadigol eu harneisio i bwrpasau celfyddyd.

Ond o feddwl am arlunwyr eraill a fu'n gweithio yn Fenis, roedd Kyffin hefyd yn gyfarwydd â'u gwaith hwythau. Arlunwyr Prydeinig ac arlunwyr o dir mawr Ewrop, arlunwyr y bedwaredd ganrif ar bymtheg a dechrau'r ugeinfed ganrif, arlunwyr fel Boudin, Whistler, Monet, Sickert, Bonington, Manet, Frank Brangwyn (un â'i fam o Glasbury, Sir Frycheiniog), Coburn (yr Americanwr) a heb anghofio Turner, roedd Kyffin wedi astudio eu peintiadau i gyd o'r union fannau hynny y bu'r meistri Guardi ac eraill yn eu peintio.

Ond fel y dywedais, 1950 oedd blwyddyn y gweledigaethau mawr i John Kyffin, pan y gwelodd ac y cyffyrddodd (fel petai) waith gwreiddiol cewri brodorol Fenis.

Y Gamlas Fawr / The Grand Canal

Santa Maria della Salute – Fenis / Venice

Yolanta

Ceffyl yn Lle Cul / Horse at Lle Cul

Dyn a Cheffyl yn yr Anialdir / Man and horse in the desert

Machlud dros Dyffryn Camwy / Sunset over Dyffryn Camwy

Y Teulu Reynolds / The Reynolds family

Norma Lopez

Brychan Evans

Euros Hughes yn dyfrhau ei gaeau / Euros Hughes irrigating his fields

Gwartheg duon Cymreig / Welsh Blacks

Ffermwyr dan y grib / Farmers below the ridge

Storm Trearddur / Storm at Trearddur

Ffermwr a gwartheg / Farmer and Cattle

Moelwyn Bach

Kyffin yn Nant Peris / Kyffin at Nant Peris

Gwyddai Kyffin am hanes Fenis, hanes a gofnodwyd mor ddisgrifiadol wych gan Gymro arall o Ogledd Cymru, sef O. M. Edwards, Cymro o Gwm Cynllwyd, Llanuwchllyn a bod yn fanwl. Fel hyn y disgrifiodd O. M. Edwards Fenis yn ei lyfr *Tro yn yr Eidal*:

"Cyn diwedd y bymthegfed ganrif, yr oedd Venice yn eithaf ei gallu a'i gogoniant. Yr oedd yr hen Roeg ac ynysoedd y Canoldir yn eiddo iddi yn y dwyrain, ac yr oedd y gwastadedd o gylch genau'r Po, gyda Phadua a Verona gadarn arno, wedi ei feddiannu ganddi yn y gorllewin. Trwy ddewrder mewn rhyfel, trwy dalent at fasnach, trwy gyfrwysdra dichellgar, daeth Venice yn allu mor gryf â Ffrainc neu'r Almaen, a dechreuodd freuddwydio am wneud ei hun yn ymherodres y byd fel y bu Rhufen, gyda brenhinoedd yn weision a'r Pab yn gaplan iddi.

Heblaw ei thiriogaeth eang — ei phorthladdoedd, ei hynysoedd, a'i gwastadeddau yr oedd cyfoeth ei masnach ymron yn anghredadwy. Yr oedd llenni tai ei thlodion o sidan, eu llestri o arian, a'u haddurniadau o aur coeth. Ac am ei chyfoethogion, y mae pob palas sydd ar lan y Canal Grande yn gartref teilwng i frenin. Yr oedd holl farsiandïaeth y byd yn pasio drwyddi, a thrysorau'r ddaear yn aros yn ei chynteddoedd. Gwlân defaid yr Hispaen a gwlân geifr Angora, haearn yr Almaen a phres Hyngari, peraroglau Arabia a sidan Bengal, pupur ynysoedd y dwyrain a pherlau'r India, aur Affrig a sinamon Ceylon gellid gweled marsiandïaeth pob gwlad ar y Rialto ac o flaen Eglwys Farce o Ddenmarc i'r Sahara, o Loegr i'r India, gellid gweled brethyn lliw a gwydr Fenis; gwyddai ei marsiandïwyr beth i'w anfon i bob gwlad — cadwyni aur a thannau ffidlau i Ffrainc, canhwyllau cwyr i'r Sbaenod defosiynol, gorchudd sidan i'r Negroes, addurniadau gwydr i frenhinesau barbaraidd y gogledd. Yr oedd enw Venice ym mhob gwlad; ac yr oedd ei llew, llew Marc, yn sefyll ar golofn mewn trefydd dirifedi, i ddangos eu bod wedi cymeryd iau'r weriniaeth falch arnynt."

Dyma oedd magwrfa celfyddyd Fenis. Dan yr amgylchiadau hyn y blagurodd artistiaid y ddinas ac y cyfranasant hwythau yn eu tro i wneud y ddinas yr hyn ydoedd. Cyfoeth y marsiandïwyr a alluogodd unigolion ac urddau Fenis i gomisiynu peintiadau olew yn bortreadau ac yn dirluniau ac yn ffrescos eglwysig, ac a wnaeth ac a wna Fenis yn ganolfan gelfyddydol o bwys.

Un o anturiaethwyr mawr Fenis oedd un o deulu'r Polo, sef Marco Polo un a grwydrodd yn enw'r weriniaeth cyn belled â llys y Mongoliad hwnnw Kublai Khan. Gwyddom fod Kyffin yn gallu adrodd cerdd fawr Coleridge i Kubla Khan, cerdd a ddysgodd yn yr ysgol yn yr Amwythig, ysgol gyda llaw, y bu Coleridge ynddi hefyd.

Rydw i am awgrymu fod yr ymweliad cyntaf yma â Fenis yn 1950 wedi rhoi 'top lein' i Kyffin ar gyfer ei yrfa hir a llwyddiannus fel arlunydd, fel portreadwr ac fel peintiwr tirluniau, ac yn arbennig felly fel peintiwr dŵr mewn olew. Fe ddaliodd Kyffin liw dyfroedd a chamlesi a *lagoon* Fenis yn berffaith. Credai Kyffin fod Fenis a'i chrefftwyr wedi dylanwadu'n drwm ar ddatblygiad peintio tirluniau.

A dyma fo, mab Essyllt a Henry Inglis, ar ben ei hun yn drachtio'n drwm o wareiddiad dieithr cyffrous, a'r lliw a'r llun a'r dŵr yn dawnsio o flaen ei lygaid (ond ddim mewn haul llachar). Does syndod yn y byd fod y ddinas wedi bod yn ganolog ar sgrîn ei feddwl o 1950 hyd 2004. Bu Kyffin eilwaith a thro yn Fenis —yn 1963, 1975 ac yn 1979. Wedi ei ymweliad yn 1979, cynhaliodd ei arddangosfa gyntaf o'i beintiadau o Fenis yn Oriel y Tegfryn ym Mhorthaethwy,

Sir Fôn, a phrynwyd nifer o'i beintiadau o'r arddangosfa honno gan Syr Idwal Pugh, y Cymro a ddaeth yn ombwdsman y Llywodraeth yn San Steffan. Ond mi wn pa nifer bynnag o droeon mae dyn yn mynd i Fenis, fedrwch chi ddim cael digon o'r ddinas. Ydi, mae'r llun ar sgrîn y meddwl ond mae'n rhaid adnewyddu'r profiad yn aml, mor aml â phosib, fel bod y llun ar y sgrîn yn berffaith glir, yn sinemasgopig, yn 3D ac yn aroglorama!

Gwyddai Kyffin hefyd am gymaint o agweddau gwahanol ar Fenis. Trafodai bensaernïaeth yr adeiladau, e.e. gwaith y pensaer Palladio y mae llawer o'i waith i'w weld yn Vicenza a chynllunwaith ei fynachlog wych San Giorgio Maggiore, a beintiwyd gan Kyffin.

Rhannai ei wybodaeth fanwl am nifer o gerfluniau'r ddinas fel gwaith mawreddog y cerflunydd mawr Andrea del Verrochio — y cerflun efydd o'r condottieri Bartolomeo Colleoni yn falch, yn hy, yn heriog ar gefn ei geffyl — a byddai Kyffin yn cofio mai felly gwelodd o ddynion y Wladfa yn marchogaeth eu meirch yn dalog ar eu ceffylau smart. Bwriadodd Bartolomeo Colleoni y cerflun yma i goffáu ei enw a dymunodd ei weld yn y Piazza canolog ger Eglwys Sant Marc, ond ger Scuola San Marco gosodwyd y cerflun efydd yn derfynol. Ymladdwr oedd proffesiwn Bartolomeo a chyfrannodd arian sylweddol i Ddinas Fenis, h.y. i'r weriniaeth. Mynnodd y cerflun i glodfori ei enw. Ac nid dim ond cerflunydd oedd y Verrochio hwnnw, ond arlunydd a gweithiwr mewn aur ac arian. Ond yr hyn a'i anfarwolodd ac a'i cododd ar bedastl yn ogystal â'i ddoniau cynhenid oedd mai ef oedd athro cyntaf gŵr nid anenwog o'r enw Leonardo o bentref Vinci ger Fflorens — ie, neb llai na Leonardo da Vinci.

Un o'r peintiadau yr ymserchodd Kyffin ynddo, ac y soniodd lawer amdano, oedd gwaith aruthrol Tintoretto yn y Scuola di San Rocco, yn Fenis — ysgol oedd yn ganolfan elusennol i'r amddifad ac i'r cleifion. Cyfres o beintiadau pwerus oedd y rhain, yn portreadu golygfeydd Beiblaidd. Dywedwyd am beintiad Tintoretto o'r Croeshoeliad "Does bosib nad oes yr un llun sengl arall yn y byd yn cynnwys cymaint o ddynoliaeth — mae popeth ynddo".

Cyflawnodd Tintoretto y rhan fwyaf o'i waith arlunio yn Fenis a'r cyffiniau — fe'i galwyd yn Tintoretto gan mai gwaith ei dad oedd lliwio defnyddiau (y gair Eidaleg *tintore* — lliw).

Soniai Kyffin am gelfyddyd Fenis gydag arddeliad. Roedd yn ei elfen, yr athro celf *par excellence* yn rhannu ei wybodaeth heb unrhyw arlliw o «dwi'n wybodus am gelf» ond yn hytrach trafodai gelfyddyd fel rhan o sgwrs naturiol. Roedd hyn yn ail natur iddo ef a chymerai yn ganiataol fod hyn yn ail natur person y sgwrsiai ag e hefyd. Fel athro da, ni wnâi i neb deimlo'n dwp neu'n anwybodus ond yn hytrach cyflwynai wybodaeth heb groesholi.

Hyd yma rydw i wedi bod yn trafod yr hyn ddigwyddodd yn y bymthegfed ganrif— gydag un naid i 1888 efo O. M. Edwards.

Gadawn hyn oll a gadael Marco Polo a Kublai Khan a dychwelyd bellach i Fôn, i Bwllfanogl a Llanfair P.G. a galwadau a gofynion yr unfed ganrif ar hugain!

Mae'n fis Mai, 2004, Mai 21 a bod yn fanwl. Mae Cwmni teledu annibynol Fflic a'i gadeirydd / cynhyrchydd blaengar Gwenda Griffith yn mynd i wireddu breuddwyd o fynd â Kyffin i Fenis ar gyfer rhaglen deledu wedi ei chomisiynu gan BBC Cymru/Wales.

Fi oedd ymgynghorydd y rhaglen ond roedd gen i swyddogaeth lawer pwysicach na hynny — y fi oedd gyrrwr personol Kyffin ar gyfer y daith — ac yn ddiweddarach, yng ngeiriau Kyffin ei hun, 'y peilot' — gair pwrpasol iawn ar gyfer taith awyren a chamlas i Fenis!

Cefais seiadau hyfryd â Kyffin ar yr aelwyd ac yn Nhafarn y Penrhos yn Llanfair P.G. yn trafod y posibiliadau ar gyfer y rhaglen. Byddai ffilmio yn ardal Cader Idris, ardal y Cnicht yn Eryri, yn South Stack ym Môn, yn ymarferol ac yn bosibl. Byddai Kyffin yn rhydd i ddewis yr union leoliadau fel y mynnai, ond roedd un rhan o'r jigso gweledol angen ystyriaeth fanwl — Fenis. Oedd hi'n bosibl — yn ymarferol — yn wyneb cyflwr iechyd Kyffin ar y pryd i drafeilio i ddinas y camlesi? Doedd o ddim yn siwr. Gwyddwn un peth o'm hymwneud ag e dros gyfnod o ddeg mlynedd a'r hugain — os mai 'na' oedd yr ateb — yna 'na' fyddai hi ac ni fyddai fy holl hyfforddiant cysylltiadau cyhoeddus mewn twristiaeth, teledu a'r sectorau masnachol, y banciau a ballu — yn cyfri am affliw o ddim. Ni fyddai waeth i mi ddychwelyd i Gwm Cynllwyd a cheisio gwastatáu llechweddi geirwon Bwlch y Groes efo rhaw fawn!

Wrth i Kyffin a minnau ystyried llyfnder y cawl yn ein powlenni yn Nhafarn y Penrhos yn Llanfair P.G. ryw brynhawn, a'r ager a godai o'r powlenni yn uno a niwloedd amhendantrwydd (os ydych chi'n deall yr hyn sydd gennyf) a minnau'n tanlinellu a phwysleisio rhan ganolog Fenis yn y cynlluniau teledol, dyma ddatganiad gan Kyffin ei fod am ei thrio hi!

Wedi'r cyfarfod tyngedfennol yma yn Nhafarn Penrhos a sicrwydd yn teyrnasu, roedd modd symud ymlaen i wneud trefniadau pendant a dyna pam, ar Fai 22, 2004 ar yr amser ordeiniedig, gyrrais yn araf i lawr y ffordd dyllog i gyfeiriad cartref Kyffin ym Mhwllfanogl.

Roedd Pwllfanogl yn llonydd, edrychais ar fy oriawr, tri o'r gloch ar y dot, roeddwn ar amser yn berffaith! Roedd y byd i gyd yn llonydd, och a gwae, rhincian dannedd a sachliain, dinistr, gwaed y cacwn a'r cocos cochion — roedd popeth ar ben, doedd

Kyffin ddim yn mynd i ddod. Pa sawl gwaith y clywais y geiriau pan oedd Kyffin mewn gwaeledd, "Fedrai ddim mynd yno, wnewch chi ymddiheuro ar fy rhan". Ac felly dyma fi yn wynebu'r anochel, yn gwthio botwm antidote dinistr fel y gwthiais ef ganwaith yn y byd teledu, yn newid fy hun yn robot oeraidd, yn barod i wynebu unrhyw beth, hyd yn oed Gŵn Annwn yn rhuthro ataf i'm llarpio, yn rhuthro i'm darnio gyda'u dannedd miniog a'u cegau slefryd yn agored led y pen!

Chwalwyd y darlun - agorwyd y drws melyn led y pen, roedd popeth yn symud. Taerais imi glywed cerddorfa, daeth awel dyner i siffrwd yn y dail, clywais sŵn afon yn harbwr Pwllfanogl, hedfannai adar o gwmpas y car. Yno yng ngwagle'r drws, safai y maestro gyda'i het banama ar ei ben. Roedd ei *knapsack* lliw *khaki* offer peintio yng nghrog ar ei ysgwydd — a photel ddŵr blastig yn sticio allan ohono (dŵr ar gyfer peintio, nid i'w yfed!) a bag sgwâr Edwardaidd wedi ei lapio efo papur brown a chortyn a ymdebygai i gortyn beindar o'i gwmpas — pob arwydd posibl fod Kyffin yn barod am daith!

Diflannodd y gerddorfa ddychmygol a thaerais i mi glywed Bob Roberts Tai'r Felin, y Welsh Whisperer, Pavarotti, José Carreras, Tom Gwanas, Wil Tân ac MC Mabon yn canu 'Moliannwn oll yn llon' — oll gyda'i gilydd ac ar lannau'r Fenai yn fy llawenydd ecstatig.

Dychmygais weld palasau'r Gamlas Fawr yn codi fel drychiolaethau. Cerddais i gyfeiriad Kyffin gan ei gyfarch "A! Syr Williams" — cyfarchiad oedd bob amser yn destun difyrrwch rhyngom. Roeddem ar ein ffordd i Fenis, roedd y daith fawr ar ddechrau!

Wedi llwytho'r car, dechreuasom ar ein taith i Fanceinion. Yn fuan wedi cyrraedd y modurffyrdd, a'r hen gar yn chwimwth ar y tarmac, deuthum i ddeall fod Kyffin wrth ei fodd yn trafeilio'n gyflym. Cyrhaeddsom y gwesty yn Wilmslow erbyn amser te hwyr. Yn ôl y trefniant, doedd yna ddim rhuthro i fod, byddem yn aros yn y gwesty y noson honno cyn hedfan i Fenis yn gynnar y bore canlynol.

Codi'n gynnar drannoeth a'i gwneud hi am un o awyrennau British Airways, yn wir am seti gorau'r awyren arbennig honno, a phan ofynnodd Kyffin i mi yn yr awyren "Is this first class?" gellais innau ateb gydag arddeliad "Of course, for you only the best"! Taith ddidrafferth, hwylus iawn oedd honno, a chyfle am sgwrs a rhoi'r byd yn ei le. Cawsom drafodaeth hynod o ddiddorol am baratoi mapiau o'r Alpau a hynny wrth i ni hedfan drostynt. Rhyfeddai Kyffin sut ar wyneb y ddaear oedd yr arbenigwyr wedi gallu mesur popeth a hynny cyn cyfnod hedfan. Cawsom sgwrs ddiddorol hefyd am fynyddoedd y Dolomitau a dyffryn yr Afon Po a gwychder Fenis yng nghyfnod y meistri fel Canaletto a Tintoretto — ac yfwyd lot o de ar y daith.

Wedi cyrraedd maes awyr Marco Polo, roedd Gwenda Griffith, a John Hefin y Cyfarwyddwr, yno i'n croesawu. Wrth i Kyffin a minnau, a'r criw ffilmio, gerdded drwy'r giatiau diogelwch olaf, gwelodd Gwenda a John Hefin yr un olygfa ac a welais i ym Mhwllfanogl - Kyffin a'i fagiau unigryw gyda'r botel ddŵr (hen botel bop) yn sticio allan o'r bag *khaki* llwyd, ond gwelsant hefyd fy mag i, sef bag plastig mawr a'r gair Euronics arno ac enw siop drydan yn y Bala yn cael ei hysbysebu ar ei ochr.

Os oedd Gwenda a John yn disgwyl bagiau Versace neu Armani, yna fe'u siomwyd! Ond nid oedd lle i siom gan Gwenda na John wrth sylweddoli fod Kyffin ar dir yr Eidal, fod Kyffin ym maes awyr Marco Polo ac ar fin mynd i mewn i'r ddinas wyrthiol, dinas y camlesi — Venezia! Wedi gadael y maes awyr, roedd cwch modur preifat cyflym wedi ei drefnu i fynd â ni yn unionsyth ar draws y lagoon i un o westai gorau Fenis a'r byd, sef Gwesty'r Danieli, rownd y gornel fel petai o Sgwâr Sant Marc ac nid nepell o geg y Gamlas Fawr, ac o fewn tafliad carreg i hen balas y Doge — arhosfan deilwng i brif arlunydd Cymru. A bron wrth i ni gamu o'r cwch modur ar garped coch y cei wrth fynedfa ddŵr y Danieli, roedd paned o de yn ein croesawu! Ond cyn i ni gamu ar y cei, cafodd Kyffin a minnau wybodaeth ddifrifol iawn: nid oedd wedi bod yn bosibl cael yswiriant i Kyffin gan ei fod yn rhy hen ac nid oedd hi'n bosibl cael yswiriant i mi gan fy mod wedi cael triniaeth ar fy nghlun. Derbyniodd Kyffin a minnau'r newyddion mewn distawrwydd ond roedd ein hedrychiad ar ein gilydd gystal a dweud "Pwy sy'n poeni! Ryden ni yn Fenis a'r Danieli yn gwahodd!" a ni fyddai neb yn cysgu efo cyllell wedi ei chlymu wrth goes ei byjamas yn y gwesty mawreddog oedd ar fin ein croesawu — wel dyna fy ngobaith o leiaf!

Ni fedraf gyfleu yn iawn y rhyddhad a deimlais fod y meistr yn ddiogel, ei fod o yno a'i fod mewn hwyliau da, ac nad oedd y daith wedi ei lethu.

Cymaint fy rhyddhad fel y syrthiais i gysgu ar y gwely anferth yn syth ar ôl cyrraedd yr ystafell wely. Ond yn nodweddiadol o Kyffin, roedd o allan yn syth, yn sgetsio ar lan y Gamlas Fawr. Roedd o yn gwneud ei waith, yn cyflawni ei orchwylion — yn cyflawni ei ddyletswyddau i'r cynhyrchydd a'r cyfarwyddwr efo Eglwys Santa Maria della Salute ar y dde iddo, adeiladwaith y pensaer Palladio, San Giorgio Maggiore, yn syth o'i flaen a dyfroedd y *lagoon* wrth ei draed. Roedd Kyffin yn ei elfen, roedd o'n gartrefol, roedd o'n 'jacôs' — wedi'r cwbwl, onid oedd teulu un o'i gyndeidiau 'Twm Chware Teg' wedi prynu tŷ yn Fenis ac wedi trigo yn y ddinas — teulu pwerus Treffos.

Ymhlith y gwaith gorchestol wnaeth Kyffin yn ystod ei ddyddiau yn Fenis roedd ei beintiad o Eglwys San Salute — golygfa wedi ei pheintio o lan y Gamlas Fawr ger Sgwâr Sant Marc, a pheintio'r eglwys hynafol hefyd o bont yr Accademia. Gwnaeth ddarlun paratoadol o'r Gamlas Fawr mewn pensil tra roedd yn y ddinas, ac yna beintiad olew godidog ar sail yr arlunwaith dechreuol, yn ôl yn ei stiwdio ym Mhwllfanogl, yr unig waith olew ar sail yr ymweliad â Fenis ac un o'i beintiadau olew olaf— gan i beintio darluniau olew fynd yn drech nag ef wedi 2004 oherwydd ei iechyd.

Do, gweithiodd Kyffin yn gydwybodol yn Fenis. Ond fe gafwyd amser i swpera efo'r criw teledu, cyfleoedd ardderchog i Kyffin i'n difyrru efo'i limrigau cofiadwy.

> A funny old fellow called Sam
> Said "Yes I will if I can.
> If I find that I can't
> I suppose that I shan't"
> A very perplexing old man.

Rhan ganolog o'r rhaglen deledu oedd yr ymweliad yma â Fenis, *Reflections in a Gondola* – rhaglen ar y thema 'Four Fortuitous Moments in my Life'.

Dechreuodd Kyffin drwy ddewis ei fan geni — Sir Fôn. Yna'r foment dyngedfenol yn ei fywyd tra yr oedd yng Ngholeg y Slade yn Rhydychen, pan y gwelodd o beintiad Piero della Francesca 'Yr Atgyfodiad' a sylweddoli nad dim ond copïo pethau ar bapur neu ganfas oedd arlunio ond fod cariad a *mood* yn rhan o'r holl broses — sylweddoliad ysgytwol.

Dewisodd hefyd y foment pan roedd yn peintio ar Gader Idris yn 1947 — pan y meddyliodd efallai, efallai'n wir, y gallai wneud bywoliaeth drwy beintio — ac yn bedwerydd, dewisodd Fenis —

dewisodd ymweld â Fenis gan wybod mai hwn fyddai ei ymweliad olaf, drwy fod y clwy creulon cancr yn cau amdano.

Wedi i ni ddychwelyd o Fenis, darlledwyd y rhaglen. Yn ôl pob tystiolaeth, bu'n llwyddiant mawr. Perfformiodd Kyffin yn wych ymhob man yn Sir Fôn, ger Cader Idris, yn Eryri, yn Llanfrothen ac fel y soniais, yn Fenis ei hun. Roedd mor ddiymhongar, mor ufudd i'r cyfarwyddwr, mor ddiwyd. Yn dilyn y rhaglen, cyhoeddais fy llyfr *Kyffin in Venice;* llyfr yn croniclo y sgyrsiau a gefais gyda Kyffin — sgyrsiau ddechreuodd ym Mhwllfanogl ac a orffennodd yng ngwychder Gwesty'r Danieli. Tra roeddem yn y gwesty, roedd fy ystafell wely y drws nesaf i Kyffin, fel y gallwn, yn ôl y trefniant, ei ddeffro yn y bore a'i arwain yn ôl y galw i'r ystafell fwyta ac yn y blaen. Ond a dweud y gwir, doedd fawr o angen gofalwr ar John Kyffin yn Fenis, 'roedd yn effro cyn pawb, yn egnïol ac yn weithgar.

Gwn o leiaf dri pheth o safbwynt Kyffin, am yr ymweliad yma â Fenis yn 2004. Yr oedd yn falch ei fod wedi mentro ar y daith, fod ganddo ffydd llwyr yn John Hefin fel cyfarwyddwr a Gwenda Griffith fel cynhyrchydd, a'i fod yn teimlo'n ddiogel yn ein cwmni fel criw o bobol oedd am wneud ein gorau iddo — ac edrych ar ei ôl yn ei henaint, gyda gofal fel y dylem. Mawr ein braint.

Pan af o dro i dro ar daith i Fenis, ceisiaf ail fyw y munudau cysegredig a dreuliais ac a dreuliasom gyda fy arwr yn y ddinas brydferth — y ddinas yr ymserchodd ynddi — yr arlunydd a'r ddinas nad a'n angof.

Precis: O Fôn i Fenis
David Meredith

A lecture dealing with Sir Kyffin's great love and affection for the city of Venice. David Meredith traces Kyffin's numerous visits to La Serenissima, beginning in 1950 and ending with his last visit in 2004, two years before his death in 2006. This lecture shines the spotlight on Kyffin the art historian, with his detailed knowledge of the great artists of Venice: Giovanni Bellini, Veronese, Tintoretto, Titian, Canaletto, and Guardi, among others. The history of Venice and its art is intertwined with details of the spectacular architecture of the city – details an art master like John Kyffin Williams loved to share with others. Fittingly for a television executive, David Meredith concludes his lecture with Kyffin's televised visit to Venice, when he glided down the Grand Canal in a decorative gondola, seeing the sights, the villas, the bridges, the churches and Palladio's monasteries.

Ganed **David Meredith** yn Aberystwyth yn 1941 yn bedwerydd plentyn i J. E. ac Elizabeth Meredith. Mae'n byw bellach yng Nghwm Cynllwyd, Llanuwchllyn. Ef yw cadeirydd Ymddiriedolaeth Syr Kyffin Williams.

Yn dilyn cyfnod fel athro Cymraeg ail iaith yng Nghaerdydd yn y chwedegau, fe'i penodwyd yn Swyddog Rhanbarthol, ac yna'n Swyddog Hysbysebu a Gwerthiant, gyda'r Bwrdd Croeso i Gymru.

Bu'n Bennaeth y Wasg a Chysylltiadau Cyhoeddus i gwmnïau teledu HTV Cymru/Wales ac S4C. Yn ddiweddarach daeth yn

Brif Weithredwr ar ei gwmni cysylltiadau cyhoeddus ei hun, 'M' David Meredith.

Dyfarnwyd gwobr y Gymdeithas Deledu Frenhinol (1997-98) iddo am ei gyfraniad at deledu yng Nghymru. Ef hefyd oedd Cymrawd cyntaf BAFTA Cymru (2001). Fe'i urddwyd i'r wisg wen yn yr Orsedd yn Eisteddfod Genedlaethol Y Bala (2009). Mae'n gyn-aelod hefyd o Gyngor ac Ymddiriedolaeth Llyfrgell Genedlaethol Cymru.

Yn awdur ac yn ddarlledwr, cyflwynodd raglen deledu ar fywyd a gwaith Syr Kyffin Williams (1978) yn Saesneg ar HTV dan y teitl *Artists – Kyffin Williams*, ac yn y Gymraeg ar S4C yn dwyn y teitl *Arlunwyr – Kyffin Williams*. Bu hefyd yn ymgynghorydd ar raglen deledu Fflic / Boom Cymru, *Reflections in a Gondola* (2004), lle bu'n trafod ymweliad olaf Syr Kyffin â Fenis.

Mae'n awdur nifer o gyfrolau am fywyd a gwaith Syr Kyffin: *Kyffin in Venice* (2006), *Bro a Bywyd* (2007), *Kyffin Williams – His Life, His Land* (2008), *Obsessed* (2012), a *Golau ar y Gamlas, Drawn to the Light* (2013).

Kyffin, Venice, &
the Spirit of Place

Jan Morris

It's ironic, I suppose, if not rather rude, that I've chosen to make the centrepiece of this talk honouring Sir Kyffin Williams a painting by Sir Kyffin Williams that is not in the Kyffin Williams Gallery. Amidst this marvellous collection of his works, I have to go and choose one that isn't there. However, you can see the picture here in Oriel Ynys Môn if you want to, because it's on the jacket of David Meredith's book *Kyffin in Venice*, which is on sale in the gallery shop – and actually, since the picture's on the jacket, you can look at it without buying the book – oh, but I really shouldn't say that!

My own favourite pictures of Kyffin's are not generally landscapes. I rather go for his fascinating portraits, of humans as of animals. The picture I'm going to talk about, though, is a landscape, or a waterscape anyway, which he painted in Venice in 2004, towards the end of his life. You might not think, either, that I would choose, out of all of his work, a painting not of Wales, or of Patagonia, but of Venice. I suppose it is true to say that Venice is the most unremittingly portrayed city in the history of the world – so far! A million pictures have been painted of its incomparable scenes, a hundred undeniable masterpieces, a thousand boring old masters listed in guide books and dutifully peered at in dim-lit chapels, ten thousand amateur watercolours produced every year, not to mention the limitless mass of instant photographs and movies! You might really think the inspiration of the old place would be beginning to wane. After all, by now don't we all know what the Grand Canal looks and feels like?

But no, we don't. We know more or less what it looks like, perhaps, but we can't say what it feels like, because of course it may *feel* different to each one of us. Even to Venice, that most familiar of all spectacles, sensibilities respond in different ways, and to my mind one of the strangest and most compelling responses of all to the presence of Venice has been Kyffin's strikingly idiosyncratic interpretation, painted seven years ago now, of – yes! – the Grand Canal.

It's a study in blues, greys, and ochres, painted from a viewpoint somewhere between the Accademia and the Rialto bridges. John Hefin, who was with Kyffin when he worked on it, told me that he did it in a kind of withdrawn, contemplative spell. I suppose I have in my library at home a few hundred paintings of the Grand Canal – in reproduction, I mean – and not one of them is remotely like this remarkable picture of Kyffin's. It is a deadpan kind of picture. The canal looks as though it might be frozen, and the sparse traffic on it – a solitary gondola, a couple of indeterminate skiffs – seems motionless. The sky is a dark, rather surly kind of blue. The water, though not rough, seems oddly perturbed, just as it does in some of his Welsh seascapes. The majestic avenue of palaces looks utterly lifeless, and the only recognizable sign of humanity in the picture is the blurred figure of the oarsman in his otherwise empty gondola. The picture is entirely Kyffin. No other influence or relationship is apparent. It is his alone.

Well, studying this beautiful and unusual thing, combining as it were the personalities of visionary artist and legendary place, makes me think once more about contacts between people and cities. I've been thinking and writing for most of my life about this particular relationship, which is sometimes antagonistic, sometimes amiable, sometimes, in fact, symbiotic; Kyffin meeting Venice seems to me an especially intriguing case study. The inspired and dedicated artist is, to my mind, the supreme example of human evolution; the city, the ultimate physical creation of mankind. Kyffin was Kyffin, Venice was, well, Venice – La Serenissima.

The picture I'm talking about doesn't in fact represent Kyffin's original contact with Venice – he had known the city for years when he painted it, and in fact his family had once owned a house there. But he tells us in one of his books that his very first impression of Venice, when he was in his thirties, was not one of brilliance and majesty, but of the light of Venice, reflected light in particular. He wrote of Venice that, 'The sky became leaden and the buildings rode silver above the light-grey water.' The colours have changed rather, but the emotions of the picture I'm talking about, painted nearly fifty years later, are recognisably the same. Like it or not, first impressions are indelibly printed upon the sensibility of any visitor to any city – and most of all, perhaps, upon the sensibilities of newcomers to Venice. And not only are we affected by our first dazzling sight of the place, we are likely to be influenced by the circumstance that's brought us there. In Kyffin's case, it was part of a first, intoxicating excursion among the artistic marvels of Europe, and there is a self-portrait showing him, weighed down with his painting gear, in a floppy old coat and baggy trousers, looking the very picture of a wandering Bohemian. More often, of course, it's a honeymoon break that introduces people to Venice. Sometimes it's a break to get over a divorce. Sometimes it's a passion for culture, sometimes just a tempting cut-rate offer from a tourist company.

In my case, as in many others', it as war that first brought me to Venice, and I remember as if it were yesterday the events that introduced me. It was at the very end of the Second World War. My regiment of the British Army, the 9th Lancers, was encamped in the valley of the Po, waiting to be shipped out to the Middle East. One day I was summoned to the tent of my commanding officer, whom incidentally some of you may remember. He was Jack Price of Rhiwlas, at Bala, a delightful man and the very model of a regular cavalry colonel. Well, he received me courteously, as always, although I was only a very undistinguished and indeed remarkably un-military sort of lieutenant, and he seemed to me rather apologetic. It was like this, he said. He was very, very sorry to have to give me some bad news. I was going to be detached from the regiment for a couple of months, because of the logistical needs of higher command. I needn't worry, he hastened to add,

I'd be back with the 9th in time to go with them to Palestine, and indeed he wanted me to become the regimental intelligence officer; but in the meantime, well, there it was, it was a rotten thing to have to do, but he had no choice: I had to leave the proud 9th Lancers and go off – wait for it – to help run the recently commandeered motor-boats of Venice.

Tears did not run down my face, and it turned out to be one of the best presents I ever had, making me in the end a sort of honorary member of Venice and giving me profound pleasure for the rest of my days. I found myself living, with a similarly ill-used subaltern from the Queen's Bays, in the requisitioned palace of a diplomat on the island of Giudecca, on the very edge of the lagoon, and I can remember my initial responses exactly to this day. Venice was a defeated city, shabby, forlorn, half-deserted. It was unutterably beautiful, I thought, but what I found most beautiful of all about it, colouring my responses from that day to this, was its pervading sense of melancholy.

It isn't very melancholy now, but still even at its most garish or hedonist – even when it is so overwhelmed with tourists that one can hardly move – even as I lean against a pillar listening to the sickly café orchestras in the twilight of the Piazza – even as I sip prosecco with my scampi thermidor and zabaglione at Harry's Bar – even then, that old delicious strain of *tristesse* loiters somewhere in my mind.

And it loiters a little too, I feel, in this picture of Kyffin's, in an element of blank or muffled expectancy. Perhaps this is historical heredity, or even evolution. For generations before his and mine, ever since the collapse of the Venetian Republic, people from these islands had looked to Venice as an emblem of lost greatness, a reminder of what their own proud empire might one day become, when their captains and kings had lost their pre-eminence – for, as Wordsworth had told them, 'men we are' – speaking for himself, of course! – 'and must grieve, when even the shade of that which once was great has passed away.' The English, when they went to Venice, painted it or wrote about it, often grieved with an ecstatic kind of melancholy, and perhaps some of that emotion had been passed down the genes to Kyffin, and to me as I wandered the pale and dappled Venice of my youth.

I suppose most responses to the city in 1945 were very different – not half so soppy. Venice was physically almost untouched by the war, and seemed not just wonderful in itself, but a first promise of better times to come. My military duties were not onerous, when dear Jack Price sent me there, and one of the most pleasant of them was escorting very senior British officers up the Grand Canal in one of our requisitioned motor-boats to their requisitioned quarters at the Danieli Hotel – where Kyffin himself was to stay when he painted his picture more than half a century later. Few of these mature and well-worn veterans had ever been to Venice before, and they had been fighting a hard war for years. They were hardly bundles of joy. They usually returned my welcome salute at the quayside with tired and unsmiling formality, but as we chugged up the Grand Canal, it was a delight to see their grizzled, warlike faces soften as we passed, one by one, beside the many prodigies, up the miraculous canal, under the Rialto bridge, and into the wide, sun-swept lagoon – their attitudes becoming gentler and kinder, happier and younger until, when we arrived at the hotel and they disembarked upon its landing stage, they would often return my farewell salute with frank and boyish laughs of sheer pleasure. I thought they ought to tip me, really.

Countless strangers have recorded for posterity their first impressions of Venice, and they have not all been stimulated. Basically, of course, newcomers have been just plain staggered that such a place could exist at all. The Venetians lived just like seabirds, a sixth century visitor recorded, and fourteen centuries later the humourist Robert Bailey was not being entirely humorous when he cabled to his editor in New York, 'Streets full of water. Please advise.' Some people have been instantly bewitched by Venice, in an almost sexual way. Others have felt let down by it. Evelyn the seventeenth century diarist, for instance, thought even the Basilica of San Marco 'dim and dismal.' Mark Twain, on the other hand, cheerfully likened the basilica to a 'vast warty bug taking a meditative walk.' A few people have detested the place from the very start, or have claimed to detest it – most famously D.H. Lawrence, who called it an 'abhorrent, green, slippery city.'

Well, it takes all sorts, and of them all, the one who reminds me most of Kyffin is Charles Dickens, who went to Venice in 1870 and wrote an essay about it that expresses, I like to think, some of the same ambiguous questioning that I sense in Kyffin's Grand Canal. It really was Dickens' first visit to the city, and when he came to write the piece, it was a misty, nebulous, cloudy sort of essay, steeped in a special kind of silence, almost like a dream. It left its subject unidentified until the very last sentence – 'I have, many a time, thought since of this strange Dream – this Dream upon the water; half-wondering if it lie there yet, and if its name be Venice.' For me, Kyffin's empty Grand Canal is something like a half-awake dream, too – not a celestial Venetian dream, like the ones Turner painted, but a dream almost in monochrome, that makes you wonder if you sleep or wake, or if it lie there yet.

Of course, first impressions are tempered as the years go by. Sometimes a place we adored when we were young turns out to be a hell-hole later – and vice-versa. As a city buff, I am often asked what my un-favourite city is, and I invariably reply, without a second thought, Indianapolis. The reply always amuses people. Mind you, I haven't yet said it to anyone *from* Indianapolis. But it's really very unfair of me, anyway. I've only been to the place once, for a single night back in 1953, and my bigotry is based entirely upon a first impression from long, long ago – it's probably a lovely place, really, and my responses to it today might be totally different. For quite apart from the passage of time, the advance of age inexorably alters our civic perceptions. It sometimes diffuses them, sometimes distorts them, sometimes gives them a new truth.

Kyffin was 32 years old when he first went to Venice, so he was already mature and experienced even when he originally saw the place. But anyway, I don't think a young man, not even a young Kyffin, could have painted his Grand Canal picture as he did half a century later, when he was 86. Its mysterious quality is instinct with experience, and with a profound suggestion of inner meaning. *Hiraeth*, possibly – he always said he painted in Welsh. Perhaps it has something to do with the fact that, as he wrote somewhere else, because of his epilepsy, he had 'always been an observer, looking into the real world and sensing that he was not part of it.' It's also as if he knows something we don't know, or is at least looking for something we haven't been told about. But then Kyffin was an artist and a seer. Generally speaking, I think we have to admit, age tends to blunt those first heady emotions of revelation. I fear the more rheumatic of those elderly generals of mine were not excited by their first experience of Venice in the same was as Kyffin must have been, and were readier for Harry's Bar than they were for lonely, sentimental introspections, like me.

I note that Kyffin, during his 86-year-old visit, painted from a gondola, an exquisite but ruinously expensive means of transport. Age might not have dulled his emotions, but it was perhaps beginning to deny him the use of the vaporetto, the inescapable waterbus of Venice. Nor does that vessel appear in his painting of the Grand Canal. The vaporetto is in itself one of the prime icons and influences of La Serenissima, and its absence from this picture is one of the instruments of its strange stillness. A Grand Canal without a vaporetto on it is like an albino, as it were, reminding me again of Dickens' peculiarly Venetian sort of silence.

Actually, I must tell you, I am not an eager vaporettist myself, hideously crowded to the gunwales as the little ships generally are. During my army days in Venice, I had motor-boats at my disposal, and later I had a boat of my own there. This so spoiled me for the vaporetto that for several decades, whenever I arrived at the railway stations, I invariably hired a water taxi, almost as expensive as a gondola, to take me up the Grand Canal. It was not until 2006 that I first boarded a number 2 vaporetto instead. This was my partner Elizabeth's idea. She's more economical than I am. We lurched slowly away among the sardine crowd on the open deck – all the seats were full – lugging our bags with us, cheek by jowl with the tourist mass, and lo, before we reached the Rialto, someone had robbed me of all my worldly wealth.

I didn't awfully like Elizabeth that evening, as we trudged across the city to report our loss to the carabinieri. I didn't much *like* her, but of course I *loved* her, as I've loved her for sixty years and more. And with cities as with people, there is a difference between liking and loving. I'm not at all sure whether, contemplating Kyffin's Grand Canal picture, you would think he much liked the place – it really doesn't look very inviting – but I don't think you'd doubt that he loved it. (As, indeed, he did, especially in that particular gentle light – because of his epilepsy, he couldn't see properly in brighter sunlight.)

I myself shall always *love* Venice, but I think I stopped entirely *liking* it about ten years ago, when they removed from the façade of the Basilica the noble golden horses of St Mark, looted from Constantinople in the Fourth Crusade, and replaced them with dull and loveless replicas. They say it was necessary for conservational reasons, and the real horses are now in a museum room behind, but for me it marked a historical and aesthetic watershed. It was the moment, I thought, when Venice finally gave up being a real living, working city of unbroken tradition, imperial tradition, and reconciled itself to being fundamentally a museum – the most extraordinary of all museums, certainly, but still to my mind no longer a genuine expression of human life, faith and aspiration. I used to be tempted, sometimes, to wish the place would just sink into the lagoon, ending its long story with a colossal splurge or gurgle of romance. Now I am more or less reconciled to its present status as probably the prime pleasure-destination of the whole world, but I cannot claim I always like it anymore.

Of course, the relationship between human being and city fluctuates down the years – it's as fickle as any other relationship. All of us age; cities too. Our functions change, like Venice's, and so do our personae, sometimes dramatically. Kyffin's eye, and Dickens' too, might see through the outer screen of a city to its unchanging inner meaning, that special silence, that haunting light, but most of us see our cities plain, just as they appear. I would guess that a majority of visitors nowadays think what a nightmare they have entered, when they arrive at Venice for the first time, having been chivvied by their tour group leader into the jam-packed Piazza San Marco – a beautiful nightmare, of course, but hardly a vision of paradise.

Cities can change their character, and so can we. In 1962, I first set foot in the city of Sydney, in Australia, and I did not like it at all. I was working for *The Guardian* in those days. I was young and brash, and I did not mince my words. The origins of Sydney, I wrote, were unsavoury, its history was disagreeable to read, its temper was course, its organisations slipshod. Its suburbs were hideous, its politicians were crooked, its buildings were either dull or distasteful, it was frigid at the soul, short of kindness, and cruelly aloof; its people were full of reproach, sneer, and grumble, and its society ladies habitually looked steely, scornful, accusatory and plebeian, as though they were expecting you to pinch their tight-corseted behinds.

And all that in one essay. That was me then, showy and full of myself. I don't think Kyffin ever went to Sydney, but I suspect his first response would have been far more temperate than mine. He would have instantly sensed, as I later did myself, the underlying fugitive beauty of the city – or he might have responded as the Cornish poet Charles Causley instinctively did when, in 1945, he first sailed into Sydney harbour as a young seaman on a Royal Navy aircraft carrier. His response was almost mystical. He likened the scene to an 'old forgotten fable...the snow-goose descending on the still lagoon, the trees of summer flowering ice and fire, and the sun coming up on the Blue Mountains. Oh, Sydney! I shall never forget you on that crystal morning!'

As a professional in the field of travel, I long ago devised a system called the Smile Test. This consisted of grinning ingratiatingly and relentlessly – unnervingly, I suppose – at passers-by in the street, and trying to deduce from their responses something of a city's character. Many people disqualified themselves from the start of my test because they simply declined all eye contact. They were so shaken by my advances that they had no time to register a response before we had passed each other. Some looked back at me with a blank but generally amenable expression, as though they would return a smile if they knew it was expected of them, and were quite certain that my smile was intended for them and not somebody else behind. A few could only just summon up the nerve to offer a little upturn at the corners of the mouth. But very many people, in many of the worlds cities, did smile back instantly, instinctively, and often I really did find that this was a reasonably fair indication of a civic character in general.

I once put all this stuff in an essay about a city which had performed particularly weakly in the Test, and whenever I go back there somebody is sure to ask me, rather grimly, 'How're we doing in the Smile Test?' I generally offer them, in response, a nervous smile of my own.

I suppose when I do the Smile Test I am really looking for what they used to call the *genius loci*, the spirit of the city, which is far more apparent in some cities than it is in others – I can't remember how powerful it was in Indianapolis, but it certainly seems to have affected me. Actually, my search for it, the smile apart, is usually quite passive. All my life I've obeyed two precepts of travel. One is from the Bible: 'Grin like a dog, and run about the city.' The other is from E.M. Forster, who wrote that the best way to experience a city was to 'wander aimlessly around.' Certainly such insights as I do get usually come uninvited. I remember suddenly imagining, for example, lying flat on my back and bone idle on the grass beside the Mall in Washington DC, I remember imagining that the *genii loci* of that city were so vigorous that I could see them up there in the sky above me, like vapour trails crossing and tumbling and arguing around the dome of the Capitol! And I stumbled all unsuspecting, years ago, upon the *genius loci* of St Petersburg, where it's been extremely busy for several hundred years. I was wandering the streets there in the footsteps of the civic laureate Dostoevsky. It was terribly muddy and slushy, and one morning I slipped in the Hay Market and lay in the street for a moment, rather shaken. But bruised and filthy as I was, I was entirely cheered up when I realised that at almost the very same spot, the murderer Raskolnikov had kissed the ground of St Petersburg in the last two pages of *Crime and Punishment*. The spirit of the place was with me! Raskolnikov got up, you may remember, and went around the corner to surrender himself at a police station. I was able to comfort myself with a cup of coffee at the nearby McDonald's.

Among all the cities of my acquaintance, two have always struck me as having civic spirits of particular force and pungency. One is Venice, the other is London, and they both meant a lot to Kyffin. He lived in London for years, painted some of his greatest pictures of Wales in his studio there, loved its winding river and was excited by the bustle of the Square Mile. Venice, he simply thought from the start, was 'the most beautiful of all cities.'

London and Venice. I am fascinated by them both too, but I find their respective civic attitudes different in kind. London I always sense to be, at heart, perfectly oblivious to its visitors, unless they're profitable. It really doesn't give a damn about us. I once found myself sailing up the London river, at the end of a very long voyage, in the company of a middle-aged American lady of very pronounced Anglophile sentiments. My, how she was looking forward to seeing London for the first time: all that antiquity, and all those royal weddings! As we leant on the deck rail together, I thought I saw in my mind's eye just what she was imagining of the city – half-timbering, of course, and thatched cottages, a Canaletto kind of river, guardsmen in bearskins, Cockneys in pearly outfits, the late Princess Diana without a doubt, St Paul's Cathedral, bowler hats, old school ties – the whole panoply of English history to be laid out before her in the presence of the great city.

But London didn't even notice she was coming, and when our ship ploughed past Canary Wharf and we approached the pool of London, Tower Bridge seemed to me to be opening for us with aloof reluctance. As for the metropolis around us, it seemed to be thinking only of itself. We could just make out St Paul's, it is true, but the Tower of London – was *that* the Tower of London? – just looked like a prison, and the mass of Kyffin's exciting Square Mile was formless, colourless, punctuated by ugly skyscrapers, heaving and grumbling with traffic – the City of London looked to me the very personification of avarice. So it should look, to my mind; that's what it's for. But, 'Oh, my!' said my companion, smiling bravely. 'It's not quite what I expected.' As if London cared.

Ah, but the *genius loci* of Venice is more adaptable, more tactful, and knows better how to evaluate its human visitors. There was no ambivalence on either side, I'm quite sure, no forced smile, no shyness either, when Kyffin Williams turned up in his gondola with his brushes and his palette to paint that portrait of it. The two of them understood each other. The Grand Canal banished its traffic at Kyffin's request, the pompous palaces closed their shutters, the vaporetti hid themselves, even the sun faded a little, so as not to dazzle him. One artist greeting another, in effortless understanding – and that's just how it should be, too.

Jan Morris is a Welsh historian, author, and travel writer known for her vivid portraits of cities – notably Oxford, Venice, Trieste, Hong Kong and New York City. Following a career in journalism that included writing for both *The Times* and *The Guardian*, Morris turned to book-writing in earnest, and has since written more than forty books, as well as countless essays, articles, and reviews. She has been awarded honorary doctorates from the University of Wales and the University of Glamorgan, and is an Honorary Fellow of Christ Church, Oxford, as well as a Fellow of the Royal Society of Literature. In 2005, she was awarded the Golden PEN Award by English PEN for a Lifetime's Distinguished Service to Literature. In January 2008, *The Times* named her the 15th greatest British writer since the War. She has also featured in the Pinc List of leading Welsh LGBT figures. Morris and her partner Elizabeth Tuckniss currently reside in north Wales, between the mountains and the sea.

'Which Way to Kyffin?'
Y Manics a'r Mynyddoedd

Prys Morgan

O s oedd rhaid i Dylan 'ddechrau yn y dechrau' yn Llareggub, rhaid gwneud yr un peth gyda'r Manics a'r Mynyddoedd. Ddechrau mis Mai 2005 cyfarfu David Meredith â James Dean Bradfield wrth gyd-deithio ar y trên o Gaerdydd i Lundain. Dyma James Dean Bradfield yn dweud ei fod ef a'i wraig yn arfaethu mynd ar wibdaith i'r Gogledd ac yn dyheu am gyfle i ymweld â Kyffin ym Mhwllfanogl. Ond tybed a fyddai yno groeso iddynt? Sut yn y byd oedd cyrraedd Pwllfanogl? Dyma David Meredith yn dweud y byddai pob croeso, bid siwr, ac yna'n tynnu map, ar gornel o gefn y papur newydd, o lonydd culion Môn a'r ffordd i Bwllfanogl. Ymhen hir a hwyr aeth David draw i weld Kyffin, a dyma'r arlunydd yn dweud ei fod wedi cael y pleser yn ddiweddar o groesawu James Dean Bradfield a'i wraig, ond eu bod wedi cael cryn drafferth i ddod o hyd i'r lle ac wedi colli eu ffordd fwy nag unwaith. A dyna yn fwy na thebyg yw tarddiad cân y Manic Street Preachers 'Which Way to Kyffin?' Rwyf yn cofnodi'r peth i helpu haneswyr miwsig poblogaidd Cymru yn y dyfodol pell.

Yna, ychydig yn ddiweddarach, ym mis Medi 2006, dywedodd James Dean Bradfield wrth y Wasg fod grym arlunwaith Kyffin a'i hynodrwydd wedi bod yn gymorth i'n diffinio ni Gymry fel cenedl. Gwir bob gair, ond sut y daeth hi fod mynyddoedd Eryri wedi troi'n ddelwedd o Gymru gyfan, ac yn symbol o'n cenedligrwydd hyd yn oed i ninnau Ddeheuwyr, a'r Manics yn ein plith? Rhaid gofyn y cwestiwn oherwydd nid felly roedd hi bob amser. Cafodd y diweddar Ioan Bowen Rees gryn anhawster wrth olygu *The Mountains of Wales* i gael deunydd gan y Cymry am eu mynyddoedd, chwaethach cael unrhyw arwydd o falchder ynddynt, cyn diwedd y ddeunawfed ganrif.

Gwlad o 'barrayn mountains' oedd Cymru i John Penry yn 1593. Aeth Joseph Hucks gyda'i gyfaill S.T. Coleridge ar wibdaith trwy'r Gogledd yn 1795 gan ddweud nad oedd y Cymry eu hunain byth yn sylwi ar y mynyddoedd ysblennydd o'u cwmpas, ac aeth Coleridge (yn 1815) mor bell â dweud bod dangos prydferthwch mynyddoedd Cymru i'r Cymry fel dangos darlun i'r dall a chanu i'r byddar. Tua 1750 cyhoeddodd rhyw Ddafydd Thomas gyfres o faledi am siroedd Cymru, ac er iddo gyfeirio at greigiau geirwon a mynyddoedd yn siroedd Caernarfon a Meirionnydd, y trigolion a'u cynnyrch yw ei unig wir ddiddordeb. Ysgrifennodd Nicholas Owen dywyslyfr yn 1795 i ymwelwyr â Sir Gaernarfon, ond does fawr ganddo i'w ddweud am Eryri, dim ond, 'All is waste and Siberian solitude'. Mae'n rhaid ei fod yn un o'r Cymry cibddall, gan fod cryn nifer o deithwyr eisoes wedi bod yn mentro, yn aml yn ddigon petrus, i ddiffeithwch Siberia Gwynedd.

Tua 1700, hyd yn oed mewn cyfnod pan fyddai llenorion gwawdlyd o Saeson yn synio am fynyddoedd Cymru fel 'the fag-end of Creation' ac yn lle da i ddim byd ond i fagu newyn, byddai ambell ddaearegwr arloesol yn mynd yno i ddarganfod creigiau'n dangos datblygiadau cynharaf y Cread, ac ambell naturiaethwr yn chwilio am bysgod a phlanhigion prin y gallent eu cymharu â rhywiogaethau tebyg yn yr Alpau. Cwynodd Edward Lhuyd yn 1695 mai meddylwyr bach plwyfol yn unig oedd yn cael mynyddoedd yn wrthun. Yn 1741 dyma William Morris (un o Forysiaid Môn) yn dweud ei fod ef a'i gyfeillion wedi mwynhau hel planhigion ar ochrau'r Wyddfa. Yn dilyn y gwyddonwyr dyma'r hynafiaethwyr yn chwilio am feini hirion a hen geyrydd, ac yna daeth teithwyr yn chwilio am olygfeydd prydferth, ac ambell arlunydd fel y Cymro Richard Wilson yn gweld crandrwydd arddunol y mynyddoedd pan fyddai'n aros gyda'i berthnasau ger Caernarfon.

Daeth y bardd o Sais, Thomas Gray, i Gymru (eithr nid i Eryri) ac ysgrifennu yn 1755 ei gerdd enwog 'The Bard' am yr olaf o feirdd Cymru yn taflu ei hun i mewn i afon Conwy i osgoi plygu i'r concwerwr Edward y Cyntaf yn 1282, y cyfan yn pwysleisio mynyddoedd Cymru fel cartref rhyddid yr unigolyn yn erbyn grym y teyrn. Roedd syniadaeth Gray yn rhan o newid dwfn ym meddylfryd y Saeson, lle dechreuent edmygu'r Cymry fel cenedl yn goroesi yn encilfeydd gwylltion y mynyddoedd. Wrth iddynt chwilio am hanes a oedd yn mynd ymhellach i'r gorffennol na dyfodiad y Sacsoniaid, edmygent y Derwyddon yn gwrthsefyll y Rhufeiniaid, a Charadog yn cynnal balchder y Brythoniaid, a'r Cymry yn ceisio sefyll yn erbyn Normaniaid. Os oedd y Ffrancwyr yn gallu honni eu bod yn ddisgynyddion y Galiaid ('Nos ancêtres les Gaulois') gallai'r Saeson honni eu bod yn olynwyr hen hil y Brythoniaid. Er mor chwerthinllyd oedd y syniad ar un olwg, cafodd y Saeson gysur felly wrth iddynt frwydro'n barhaus yn erbyn Ffrainc a Sbaen. Fel mae Peter Lord wedi sylwi, gwelent y Cymry fel darn o archeoleg fyw, a buddiol felly oedd teithio i Gymru i gloddio a chwilio am hen darddiadau gorffennol Prydain.

Wedi 1770 newidiodd y llif bychan o deithwyr i Eryri yn genllif nerthol, yn arbennig felly yn y cyfnod rhwng 1793 a 1815, pan fyddai'n amhosibl i deithwyr fynd i'r Cyfandir o achos rhyfeloedd maith yn erbyn Ffrainc. Cafwyd ffyrdd newydd, gwestai a llyfrau tywys i'r teithwyr a digon o luniau iddynt brynu fel atgofion, a hyd yn oed dywyswyr i'w helpu i ddringo'r copaon, ac i bob pwrpas roedd oes y teithwyr cynnar wedi troi'n oes twristiaeth.

Ond beth am y Cymry eu hunain? A newidiodd eu hagwedd hwy? Ysgrifennodd Iolo Morganwg englyn i fynydd uchaf Bannau Brycheiniog, Ban Uchdeni neu Ben y Fan, ac er mai ar fryncyn bychan Bryn y Briallu yn Llundain y sefydlodd Iolo ei Orsedd yn 1792, buan y dechreuodd yr arfer o gynnal Gorsedd Beirdd Ynys Prydain ar gopaon Cymru megis Bryn Dinorwig. Yn 1802 ysgrifennodd William Williams Llandygái, pennaeth chwareli llechi enfawr teulu'r Penrhyn ei *Observations on the Snowdon Mountains*, lle y ceisiai brofi mai yn yr ucheldir y goroesodd bywyd cynhenid y Cymry yn ei ffurf buraf. Syniadau digon tebyg oedd gan John Blackwell, y bardd Alun, yn ei anerchiad i Eisteddfod Biwmares yn 1832, syniad rhamantaidd mai yn y mynyddoedd y cedwid Cymreigrwydd digyfnewid drwy'r oesau. Dilynodd ambell arlunydd o Gymro'r trywydd a agorwyd gan Richard Wilson, a dyma Edward Pugh yn 1816 a Hugh Hughes yn 1823, er enghraifft, yn cyhoeddi llyfrau o luniau o'u mamwlad, yn cynnwys y mynyddoedd geirwon. Eithr fe ddaeth argyfwng annisgwyl ar draws diwylliant y Cymry a wnaeth i Gymru benbaladr droi at y mynyddoedd am noddfa a chysur ar ddechrau oes Fictoria.

Enw poblogaidd (neu amhoblogaidd) yr argyfwng oedd 'Brad y Llyfrau Gleision', am fod Llywodraeth Llundain wedi cyhoeddi adroddiadau mewn cloriau gleision yn 1847 ar gyflwr addysg yng Nghymru, a'r adroddiadau yn llawn o ensyniadau haerllug a chas am ddiffygion moes a rhinwedd yn y Cymry, yn enwedig y werin derfysglyd ac annisgybledig, gan gynnwys y merched, ac yn gofyn am raglen o addysg Saesneg i wella a moderneiddio'r genedl. Cododd y llysenw ymhlith y Cymry o ddrama Brad y Llyfrau Gleision yn 1854 gan Robert Jones Derfel, ac o fewn dim daeth llu o gyfansoddiadau yn clodfori mynyddoedd Cymru, hynny yw, fel ffordd o glodfori Cymru ei hun. A allai hyn fod yn llwyr ar hap a damwain? Dyna i chi Islwyn y bardd o Sir Fynwy, heb fod nepell o fro'r Manics, yn dechrau ysgrifennu ei gerdd hirfaith 'Y Storm' yn 1854, lle mae'r bardd yn synfyfyrio ym mynyddoedd stormus Cymru. Yn 1854 y dechreuodd George Borrow gasglu deunydd at ei glasur *Wild Wales* am ei daith trwy froydd Cymraeg a mynyddig

Cymru a gyhoeddwyd wedyn yn 1862. Yn 1856 y lansiwyd ein hanthem genedlaethol 'Hen Wlad Fy Nhadau' gyda'r ail bennill yn dechrau â'r geiriau 'Hen Gymru fynyddig, paradwys y bardd'. Yn 1860 cyhoeddodd Ceiriog delyneg enwocaf y ganrif, 'Nant y Mynydd', a chyhoeddi yn 1861 ei gylch o ganeuon 'Alun Mabon', yn clodfori bywyd bugeiliol y mynyddoedd, ac yn gorffen gyda'r enwog 'Aros mae'r mynyddau mawr', lle mae'r ucheldir yn gartref i bopeth da ac oesol ym mywyd y genedl, fel yr heniaith a'r caneuon a moesau dilychwin y werin. Yn yr un flwyddyn y daeth 'Mynyddoedd Eryri' gan Gwilym Cowlyd, ac yn 1862 y cafwyd ymgais Ceiriog a Brinley Richards i ysgrifennu anthem frenhinol i Gymru, sef 'Ar D'wysog Gwlad y Bryniau, O Boed i'r

Nefoedd Wen', sydd yn dechrau yn y fersiwn Saesneg â'r geiriau 'Among our ancient mountains, and from our lovely vales', a dyna'r anthem a adwaenir fel arfer fel 'God Bless the Prince of Wales'. Yn 1863 cyhoeddwyd y llyfr diddorol *Cofiant Dafydd Rowland* sy'n sôn am y bryniau o gwmpas y Bala, gan ddangos mor iachus oedd effaith bywyd y mynydd ar fuchedd y bobl yno, ac yn 1866 y cyhoeddwyd y llyfr mwyaf arwyddocaol ohonynt oll, sef *Hynafiaethau Llandygái a Llanllechid* gan Huw Derfel Hughes, sef tywyslyfr i 'r Cymry Cymraeg iddynt fynd i 'r mynyddoedd. Yn 1868 wedyn y cyhoeddwyd cathl boblogaidd Eos Bradwen 'Bugeiles yr Wyddfa', ac yn 1873 cyhoeddwyd geiriau enwog Ceiriog i'r alaw 'Nos Galan', gan ddechrau â'r llinellau 'Oer yw'r gŵr sy'n methu caru, Hen fynyddoedd annwyl Cymru' a'r holl ffalalalala yn dilyn. Gellir gweld felly bod rhyw fath o chwyldro meddyliol wedi digwydd rhwng 1850 a 1870 i greu ffasiwn newydd am rywbeth a gellid ei alw yn 'fynyddgarwch'.

Ar lawer cyfrif, gosodwyd patrwm yn y cyfnod hwn a fyddai'n cael ei ddilyn gan genedlaethau i ddod: dyna Owen M. Edwards yn ysgrifennu *Tro Trwy'r Gogledd* yn 1907, a T. H. Parry-Williams yn ei gerddi 'Y Mynydd' (1912) ac ' Eryri' (1915), a llawer o benillion yn ymuniaethu fel llenor â'r moelydd a'r carneddau o gwmpas ei gartref yn Rhyd Ddu. Creigiau a llechi Arfon sy'n gefndir i straeon a nofelau Kate Roberts, a nofel Caradog Pritchard, *Un Nos Ola Leuad*. Cymaint yw cyfraniad llenorion Eryri i lenyddiaeh Gymraeg yr ugeinfed ganrif, nes ei bod yn anochel fod pawb sy'n darllen y Gymraeg yn ymdrwytho ym mywyd y mynyddoedd. Mae hynny'n un o'r elfennau sy'n ein denu i 'w gweld fel ein cynefin ninnau megis trwy ras a mabwysiad.

Soniwyd uchod am osod patrwm. Cafwyd cynsail yn ogystal o droi at y mynyddoedd fel Dinas Noddfa neu ddihangfa yn amser cyfyngder neu argyfwng cenedlaethol. Digwyddodd hyn i'r Saeson yng nghanol y ddeunawfed ganrif, ac yn bendant, digwyddodd i'r Cymry wrth iddynt lyfu eu briwiau a'u clwyfau wedi 'Brad y Llyfrau Gleision'. Gellid dadlau bod y Cymry wedi dioddef argyfwng hirfaith yn ystod yr ugeinfed ganrif, wrth i rai o hen bileri eu Cymreigrwydd fel y Capel neu'r Heniaith ddirywio mor arswydus yn ystod y cyfnod, gan orfodi'r Cymry druain i chwilio am gysur neu am arwyddion o'u parhad fel cenedl. Mae'n bosibl mai dyma sydd wedi gwthio'r Cymry — beth bynnag eu hiaith a phle bynnag y byddent yn byw — i anwylo delwedd y mynyddoedd fel lloches. Eryri yw cartref broydd Cymreiciaf y Wlad, y broydd sydd bellaf oddi wrth Loegr a'r broydd sydd fwyaf annhebyg i wastatir Lloegr. A phwy yw'r arlunydd sy'n mynegi'r tirwedd yma orau? Neb llai na Kyffin Williams. Y mae fel rhyw arlunydd llys i Eryri, fel oedd Van Dyck i lys Siarl y Cyntaf. I Gymry benbaladr Kyffin yw'r lladmerydd perffaith, yn cyfleu i'r dim y ddelwedd o amddiffynfa fynyddig y gallwn ei gwisgo fel bathodyn ar ein lifrai fel Cymry.

Nid mater o dirlun neu gefndir mynyddig yn unig ydyw: mae'r bugeiliaid a'r ffermwyr, eu cŵn a'u ceffylau a'u buchod a'u defaid, yn cyfleu pobl sy'n crafu byw yn nannedd stormydd glaw a chenllysg, eu defaid yn aml ar goll mewn lluwchfeydd o eira mewn cilfachau a cheunentydd dan y copaon. Mae cymaint o ddelweddau poblogaidd Kyffin yn symbolau graffig o ymdrechion y Cymry i oroesi, a hynny i ni ar draws Cymru gyfan. Mae bywyd un pegwn o'r wlad yn sefyll dros y cyfan, rhyw fath o synecdoche o inc a phaent. Mae hyn hefyd yn wir am ei luniau o Batagonia, lle mae'r gwladfawyr yn llwyddo rywsut ar gefn eu ceffylau i oroesi yng ngwyntoedd y paith, neu i fyny yn yr Andes, lle mae Gorsedd y Cwmwl fel rhyw Wyddfa ym mhendraw'r byd. Fan yna eto mae darluniau Kyffin fel rhyw T.H. Parry-Williams neu Kate Roberts neu Garadog Pritchard mewn paent ym mhellafoedd America.

Ar y dechrau gwelsom sut y daeth y Manics i ganu 'Which Way to Kyffin?' Ond wrth gwrs, i hanesydd y mae yna ddechrau cyn pob dechrau, ac fe ddaethom ar draws dynion fel Edward Lhuyd a Thomas Gray, Iolo Morganwg a Cheiriog ac Islwyn ac eraill yn ein hebrwng ar y daith fynyddgar hir sydd yn ein tywys yn y diwedd at Kyffin. Mae James Dean Bradfield wedi dweud bod Kyffin yn help inni i gyd i ddiffinio ein cenedligrwydd. Gwir y gair. Roedd Islwyn y bardd yn dod o Gwm Sirhywi yng Ngwent nid nepell o fro'r Manic Street Preachers, ac roedd Islwyn yn greadur cerddorol dros ben, ac mae dyn yn ffansïo rywsut y byddai wedi hoffi cân y Manics.

Mae'r oll yn gysegredig, wedi'r cyfan. Hyd yn oed y Manics.

Precis: 'Which Way to Kyffin?': Y Manics a'r Mynyddoedd

In May 2005, David Meredith drew a sketch map for his friend James Dean Bradfield to help him find his way to Kyffin's house in Anglesey. He got lost several times before being welcomed by Kyffin, and from this encounter came the Manic Street Preachers' song 'Which Way to Kyffin?' In September 2006, James Dean Bradfield said that Kyffin's landscapes helped us to define ourselves as a nation, for although we don't all come from Snowdonia, all of us regard Kyffin's work as typifying Wales.

It was wholly different in the past: in 1795 Nicholas Owen dismissed Snowdonia as 'waste and Siberian solitude'. But more appreciative views appeared during the eighteenth century, with Snowdonia's vastness being penetrated by botanists, geologists and painters such as Richard Wilson. English travellers visualised the Welsh mountainscape as a fortress that symbolised Britain's century-long wars against France and Spain.

By the mid-nineteenth century, the outsiders' views began to impress even the natives. But it was the cultural crisis of The Treason of the Blue Books in 1847 that forced the Welsh to embrace their mountains as a badge of nationhood. The pattern was set so that by the later twentieth century, with the decline of the chapel and the language as older markers of nationality, we have grasped Kyffin's landscapes as powerful symbols of nationhood.

Yr Athro Prys Morgan D.L.

Mae Prys Morgan yn Athro Hanes Emeritws ym Mhrifysgol Abertawe.

Mae'n Gymrawd o'r Gymdeithas Hanes Frenhinol, Y Gymdeithas Frenhinol a Chymdeithas Ddysgedig Cymru.

Ers 2005 ef yw Llywydd Cymdeithas Anrhydeddus y Cymrodorion. Mae wedi ysgrifennu'n helaeth ar ddiwylliant yng Nghymru, gan gynnwys ysgrifau ar arlunwyr megis Thomas Jones, Pencerrig.

Mae ei lyfr *Welsh Surnames*, yn cael ei ystyried yn glasur yn ei faes. Yn ogystal mae'n awdur ar nifer o erthyglau arbennig ar fynyddoedd Cymru.

Their Land Is Our Land

Prof. Tony Jones, CBE

Before and since Sir Kyffin Williams died, much had and has been said and written about him. There are the exhibitions, the books with excellent recollections of him by close friends, family, admirers – wonderful writing by Ian Jeffrey, Nicholas Sinclair, a beautiful collection of essays published by Gregynog Press, a terrific interview with Professor Tony Curtis, and Kyffin's autobiography, *Across the Straits*.

So when Dr Derec Llwyd Morgan asked me to prepare a presentation for the Sir Kyffin Williams Trust memorial lecture series, I was intimidated. Many knew Kyffin better than I did, and know the work better too. I live 4,000 miles away, in Chicago, so I see Wales, its artists, and Kyffin, from that different perspective

151

– not with the almost-daily intimacy of those who live here. And the last thing I wanted to do was deliver an illustrated obituary.

So this is not a scholarly disquisition, or an art-history lesson, or a dense reading of the ecology and geography of Kyffin's works; instead, my remarks are both about Kyffin and around Kyffin, seen from that great distance. I ask you to accept them simply as a fond observation about an admirable artist, by a fellow Anglesey boy. My life has taken me far from this island, but I am proud and honoured to be invited to talk about what artists try to do, what the landscape means to them, and how they try to convey that meaning.

Artists try to take you to the place they have claimed as their own, to whatever land has inspired them. To put you where they were, in that place, and bring you to the sensation of that place – what the French call *l'impression* – not simply what it looked like, but an impression of what it *felt* like. Kyffin's exploration of landscape did exactly that. How many of us now drive through Snowdonia and see it differently – in stormy weather, perhaps – and think, 'That's a Kyffin sky'? Or see shepherd and dogs working a flock and expect to see Kyffin up there with them, drawing? I will try to place Kyffin in that context, as a way of thanking him for showing us a Wales that we see every day, but that, in Kyffin's impressions, is revealed to us anew.

A couple of years ago, I visited the home of one of the greatest landscape-inspired artists – the studio and famous gardens of Claude Monet at Giverny, outside Paris. I discovered, surprisingly, that there is not a single painting by Monet to be seen there; they are all in Paris, or in major museums all across the world (including at the Art Institute in Chicago). Wandering Giverny, I thought, 'How inappropriate that here we are, surrounded by the *subject*, but there is not one example of how the inspiration of this place resulted in the great works Monet made.' Surely, I felt, this should not happen with Kyffin's work. People should be able to see the *where* of his inspiration as well as the *what* – that is, the work itself. This is what Oriel Kyffin seeks to do.

If I might advance an idea about Oriel Kyffin, it's that its future lies in not only celebrating the work of Kyffin, but in surrounding his achievement with the work of others equally inspired by the Welsh landscape. Seeing Wales by Kyffin is quite different from the perspective of a photographer like David Hurn, for example. His work explores the Mawddach Estuary, and ranges from the mathematics of sheepdog trials to wonderfully comic incidents in the landscape, like a flock of sheep waiting for a bus.

Richard Wilson in the 1700s saw Wales quite differently than Peter Prendergast did in the 2000s – and both of them saw Wales differently than Turner, or Hurn, or Kyffin. That is the joy and enduring value of Oriel Kyffin – these organic layers of artistic vision, each seam adding to the strata. All of these visions of Wales are different, and each of them is as valid as the other. Every exhibition is a revelation of something we thought we already knew.

Kyffin and I shared something that we always remarked upon: the good fortune that we came from Anglesey stock (to which, in my case, had been added a dollop of Scots.) Whenever I saw him, he'd ask, 'Where are you now?', and I'd say London, or Glasgow, or New Orleans, or Texas, or Chicago. He would answer back, 'No, you're not. Look where your feet are – you're *home*, on Anglesey.'

I took this to be a metaphor typical of his thinking. 'Home' meant the very earth on which we were standing – the ancient rock and green mantle that we called the Landscape of Anglesey and Snowdonia. The very same landscape he tried to grab and hold and study and distil and cram onto a canvas. It is possible to describe that process in a single Welsh word. What Kyffin and artists like him who render the Welsh landscape are looking for, what they are trying to capture, what they are trying to show is this: *hanfod*.

It means *essence*. The heart, the core, the most fundamental – what Jan Morris called 'the *matter* of Wales'. It is a process of boiling down, of compressing and reducing down to elemental pieces before building back up to something that represents the statement the landscape makes to you. I once told Kyffin about a great artist who had defined the artist's life as one spent defacing pieces of cloth with twigs and hair and pots of coloured grease. He laughed and agreed. And not only that, he told me, but doing it on top of some freezing mountain in north Wales, with sleet falling in the paint, thunder and lightning bashing you about the place, and rain that is hell-bent on turning your vibrant watercolour into an anaemic dribble. But artists often turn accidents into art, so I'm sure that Kyffin's ring-binder sketchbooks have accidents of nature that he's incorporated into the work – perhaps the dashing way he laid into colour and form, combining watercolour, ink and gouache all have a sense of urgency and immediacy because he was racing an impending downpour.

In the U.S., there's been a fascinating study conducted about the behaviour of people in museums. Museum visitors spend an average of eight seconds standing in front of a single painting. But I once stared at a single Kyffin painting nearly every school day for an entire year. This was long before I ever met the artist himself, but it created an early bond between us. 'My' Kyffin was an oil painting, about 5ft x 4ft, that hung in the art room of Quakers Yard Grammar School in Treharris. It was there because of an enlightened project run by the County Borough of Merthyr Tydfil to place works of art in schools. Nearly all of them were by living or recently deceased contemporary artists who worked in Wales. Incredibly, the displays even rotated. Every so often, a van would come and swap the pictures for a new set, and ours went to some other school.

Among ours was one I called 'my' Kyffin. It was a north Wales subject, painted around 1958 with a mixture of brush and palette knife, thick as pebble-dash, and it was called *Tanygrisiau*. I went to the art room every day and sat next to it (the headmaster's end-of-year letter to my family stated that, 'Anthony is not stupid and he might make something of himself if he didn't spend all his time hiding in the art room'). One day I helped the art teacher, Colin Jones, to move 'my' Kyffin so that it hung over my desk. I looked longer and harder at it than I have at any painting since.

From Kyffin I learned practical lessons in composition and how to lay down paint – in other words, what I call 'the engineering of a painting'. And years later, when I finally met Kyffin, I told him about this experience, and how much I had learned from his painting. His reply? 'No, you didn't. I've never painted a picture called *Tanygrisiau*'.

I was mystified. I explained about moving the picture and seeing his signature and hand-written title on the back, as well as his familiar initials on the front. He had no memory of it. And thus the bond of mystery joined us. We'd talk about it every time we met. When I filmed the BBC series *Painting the Dragon*, we came up to shoot a sequence with him, and the first thing he said to me was, 'Well, Anglesey boy, have you found a photo of *Tanygrysiau*?' Kyffin still couldn't remember the painting at all, one that had been so important to me.

When Derec Llwyd Morgan asked me to come and talk about Kyffin, I set about tracking that painting down. When my old school, Quakers Yard, closed, it was moved to Troedyrhiw and renamed Afon Taff. In 1972 an art exhibition was held there. I managed to find the wee catalogue of recent acquisitions they produced. It was an extraordinary collection – and among the works listed was an oil painting by Kyffin Williams called *Tanygrisiau*. But there the trail went cold. The painting has disappeared. Colin Jones, the art teacher, left teaching, I went away to college, Quakers Yard School was demolished, everyone who taught at Afon Taff school had retired…there were no stones left to overturn.

And then I got an email from Afon Taff's retired headmaster, telling me the story of a Kyffin painting discovered in the school's boiler room by the art teacher, about to be thrown into the furnace! It was saved, but the hunt continues, the mystery endures – but somewhere in Wales, someone has the great joy of looking at 'my' Kyffin every day, as I did. And they, whoever they are, are lucky people.

So what did that painting signify to me then, and what does it mean now? Kyffin's landscapes are always about the essentials. In fact, so are his portraits. They contain the essence of the land, and the people who live on it. The sky and stone, the drama and energy of the vast, untameable, and often threatening Welsh landscape – they are the same base elements as the skin and bones and clothes and character of his portrait sitters. It's all one. It's all *hanfod* – essence.

But that essence is hard to pin down, though you know it viscerally as well as intellectually. Simply put, Kyffin painted in oil, and he painted in Welsh. Back in 1960, when I was still staring at 'my' Kyffin in its place on the school room wall, artist David Bell was putting forth the idea that Wales had no visual artistic tradition. It was an erroneous thing to say then, and is proven ever more false as the years pass – by the scholarship of historians like Peter Lord, by the rigor of the critical discourse led by figures such as Iwan Bala and Sheila Houhrahan, and perhaps most especially by the growth of the number of artists who are working here. Are those artists Welsh? I suppose that depends on your definition. But they have certainly become *of* Wales – Welsh by birth, by residency, or by persuasion.

When we filmed *Painting the Dragon* and created the accompanying exhibition at the National Museum in Cardiff, I asked each of the participating artists what Wales meant to them. No matter if the artists were as different as Shani Rhys James and Ivor Davies, or Kevin Sinnott, or Clive King, or Tony Stevens – at the core of all of their answers was that Wales itself provided an experience of place that was unique and therefore critical to their work. Nowhere else could be for them what Wales was. To paraphrase the great William Turner, when he came to Wales to seek out the same landscapes that had inspired Richard Wilson – the soil is Welsh, and so should be the harvest.

Kyffin painted his Welshness as well. Though he created art in many places – Holland, France, Italy, Greece, or even Patagonia – he always claimed that in none of those countries did he find a mood that touched the melancholy found within most Welshmen – a melancholy derived from dark hills, heavy clouds, and enveloping sea mists. So whether it is Oriel Kyffin, Oriel Davies, the National Museum in Cardiff, the galleries in Llandudno or Newport – wherever – they all have a role in removing the perception that Wales offers no visual cultural tradition, and in replacing it with actual fact: that Wales is an inspirational and nurturing landscape. That it does now what it has always done, in awakening the best ideas and best expressions of those who are open to see its magic.

Kyffin and his art will forever be linked to this land he loved, and where he made his best work, in that intimidatingly jam-packed studio so rich in smells of paint, linseed oil, turpentine, Calor Gas, and the mucky brine of the Menai Straits just yards away. He dragged the vastness of the Welsh landscape through the little door of that studio, then stripped it down to skin and bones and light. In Kyffin's work there is not an ounce of fat; it's lean painting. But with that voluptuous paint trowelled onto the surface of a canvas, austerity never looked so rich.

The sheer physicality of that paint becomes a driving element in how you respond to Kyffin's landscapes. It's deep, and heavy. Sensual. Laid on thick like cream. There's no washy staining of the canvas in the Snowdonia landscapes, but bold slabs of thick oil paint layered onto the surface with palette knives. I once helped him move a large finished work in his studio, and had never previously considered the issue of the sheer weight of paint on canvas. This very weight is a part of his expression. A large tube of oil paint can weigh pounds, and he used a lot of tubes.

The paintings look so solid because they're built like brick walls – and to build a wall, you need muscle. The Kyffin I knew was genteel, courtly, elegant of phrase, affable and kindly – though not without strong opinions, sometimes waspishly expressed. I never saw that side of him, though we had differing views.

Kyffin described *himself* as an obsessive, depressive, diabetic epileptic; apprehensive, selfish, intolerant, and ruthless. This may be so, and there's no doubt that the turbulence occasioned upon him by his clinical conditions was reflected in the way he painted. I think the physical act of painting was a way of moving that turmoil from the heart and head to the hand and canvas.

So if you met the courtly Kyffin, perhaps you'd expect landscapes that were brilliantly, carefully crafted, but also academic and dispassionate. Illustrative. This was clearly not so. Kyffin the painter was a mauler, an emotional and gutsy painter. His style of painting was what we'd call in America 'in your face' – an aggressive, expressionistic handling of thick sods of paint to make a surface that is churning, restless and dynamic. There is a ferocity of execution that comes off the canvas and grabs you; it's a very physical, hands-on, almost combative sort of painting. Kyffin's work is not only about what he saw in the subject, but about the act of painting itself.

Some people, misguidedly, think that slopping paint onto a canvas, even in thick mosaic swirls, is easy enough. But palette knives, though flexible and responsive, are tricky to use. They require great skill and dexterity to utilise. But they are not only tools for ladling paint onto a surface; surprisingly, they are also drawing instruments. By turning the edge, you can scribe into the surface, or you can apply pressure and build up a line on the edge of a form. Even more pressure, and you can squeeze an underlying layer of colour until it bleeds up to the surface. For Kyffin, these were his weapons of choice in his duel with paint.

Of course, tools can sometimes have a life of their own. They can slip and create happy accidents – or disasters. They can become so honed that they'll slice right through a canvas, or a hand. Kyffin often talked about the accidents and abnormalities of his life, and he was told by a doctor that, because of epilepsy, he was already abnormal – why not take up art? Kyffin felt that, because he was not a born artist, he was able to paint in an uncomplicated manner, free from the pressure felt by someone who *knows* he is an artist and must therefore live up to that ideal. Instead, Kyffin simply considered himself a vehicle for expressing the view in front of him.

This idea should not, however, detract from the recognition of Kyffin's considerable technical skill. His dramatic use of paint is never uncontrolled. Under the 'skin' of paint is a rock-solid 'skeleton' of composition. His paintings are beautifully engineered – after all, he was trained at the Slade School in London and fully understood the mechanics of strong composition. Kyffin likened his paintings to crossword puzzles – there was only one solution, one arrangement that would fit. Though the overall effect is visceral and reactive, the passion of Kyffin's work is built upon a solid technical foundation.

An example of this is Kyffin's love of dramatic contrast. No doubt this was nurtured in part by the land in which he worked. He could stand on a sunny hill in Anglesey and stare at a snow blizzard bashing the Snowdonia hills just a few miles away. We often talked about this shared experience, we Anglesey boys, and of how this natural theatre of contrast influenced his work. Kyffin also attributed this aspect of his work to his epilepsy; he painted strong darks and lights, he said, because he craved excitement. But all of this turbulence – drawn from nature, from illness, and from Kyffin himself – was always balanced by skill and training. The apparent spontaneity of his work was always underpinned by a canny intelligence, and by a deliberate structure lurking just beneath a churning surface.

Perhaps this, too, is a contrast Kyffin would appreciate: at the National Gallery in London, hangs Gainsborough's magnificent double portrait *Mr and Mrs Andrews*. The figures are posed in the middle of a vast, flat, field in East Anglia. They are arrayed in their finest, he carrying his best rifle and she with her nicest dress and spotless shoes, accompanied by their attentive gundogs. It's the quintessential English landscape starring quintessential English gentry. A visitor to the gallery once asked historian Kenneth Clark what the two figures were doing out there in that landscape. 'Owning it,' said Clark. If you asked the same question about one of Kyffin's great landscapes of shepherds and dogs on a stormy hilltop, Kyffin might have answered, 'Surviving it.' Kyffin's way of painting, the look and style of his work, is distinctive, personal, unique – but also immediately accessible to a wide audience. A few have criticised his compositions as generic – not really of specific places, but compilations of many places that are given a single name for convenience. This is simply not so. Kyffin could reel off the names of every bump or hill in his landscapes, say when he painted them, from what compass point, in what weather. It is that very specificity that lends such an immediacy to his work. Each piece is saying to us, 'I was here in this place, and now you are too.' In Kyffin's landscapes you can smell the earth, hear the wind roaring on the hilltops and the cries of the sheep and hawks, you can feel the blinding sun, hear the crash of thunder in the boiling clouds, and smell the salty sea. They are all there, these essentials, this 'matter' of Wales, deep inside his paintings.

So let me put it this way, as a final note of appreciation for the man and the artist: I think the triumph of Kyffin's work, and why it speaks to so many so forcefully, is that Kyffin found the heart and soul of the land he saw. He captured the *hanfod*, the essence, perhaps even the DNA of the Welsh landscape, and he put it all in the paint.

Professor Tony Jones, CBE was born in north Wales, and studied as a painter, sculptor, and art historian in Wales, London, and the United States. Professor Jones has an international reputation as an arts administrator, educator and historian, as well as a consultant on higher education and the arts. He has served as both president and president-emeritus of the Art Institute of Chicago, and as the director of the Royal College of Art in London. He is honorary director of the Osaka University of the Arts, honorary professor of the University of Wales, was conferred the Austrian Cross for services to European education, and is a Fulbright Scholar. He has been awarded four honorary doctorates, was made an honorary member of the American Institute of Architects, is Senior Fellow of the Royal College of Art, London, and a Fellow of the Royal Society of Arts. Currently, Professor Jones is the director of the Kansas City Art Institute in Kansas City, Missouri.

'Ei luniad yn oleuni':
R.S. Thomas ym myd lluniau

M. Wynn Thomas

Mae gen i lun trawiadol, gwerthfawr, yn y tŷ. Ffotograff ydyw o dri gŵr adnabyddus iawn yn mwynhau cwmni ei gilydd, sef Emyr Humphreys, R.S. Thomas a Kyffin Williams. Dyma chi, yn ddi-os, bortread hanesyddol o dri o fawrion mwyaf diwylliant Cymru yr ugeinfed ganrif. Mae'n briodol ar un ystyr fod R.S. a Kyffin yno'n sefyll ysgwydd yn ysgwydd. Oherwydd yn sicr roedd cynghanedd yn bod rhwng gwaith y ddau; gwaith cynnar R.S. adeg Manafon a llunio'r cerddi am Iago Prytherch a'r tirluniau caregog, esgyrnog, tywyll a wnaeth Kyffin Williams yn eilun dosbarth canol 'Cymru'r ddinas'. Yn y cerddi cychwynnol mae R.S. yn gosod geiriau yn drwch delweddol ac ansoddeiriol ar bapur, gan eu pentyrru mewn modd sy'n cyfateb yn fras i'r *impasto* a geir yn y lluniau olew sy'n nodweddu gwaith Kyffin. Fe deimlai'r ddau ohonynt yr adeg honno mai dyma'r math o gyfrwng oedd yn addas ar gyfer darlunio gerwinder ysgythrog tirwedd mynyddig Cymru yr oedd y ddau ohonynt yn ymserchu cymaint ynddi. Ond yn araf bach, fe aeth R.S. fwyfwy i amau gwerth lluniau o'r math, ac erbyn iddo gyrraedd ei gyfnod olaf oll fel bardd ni fedrai bellach ddioddef y lluniau 'Kyffinaidd' y mynnai Bloodaxe o hyd ddewis ar gyfer cloriau ei gyfrolau. Testun y ddarlith hon yw'r newid yna a fu yn ei yrfa, er na fynnwn am eiliad awgrymu i hynny leihau ei barch at waith ei gydnabod Kyffin Williams o gwbl.

Fe ddyle fod gan R.S. grap go dda ar hanfodion celfyddyd weledol. Wedi'r cyfan, fe roedd e'n briod ag artist am hanner canrif. Pan briododd e Mildred (Elsi) Eldridge roedd hi eisoes yn un o sêr ifanc y byd celf soffistigedig yn Llundain. Ac fe roedd ei llwyddiant hi'n cael ei amlygu gan y soft-top Bentley steilus roedd hi'n hoff o'i yrru o gwmpas y ddinas. Newydd orffen ei gyrfa yn y Coleg Cerdd Brenhinol yr oedd hi, ac yno roedd hi wedi ennill sawl gwobr nodedig am ei gwaith. Yn sgil un o'r llwyddiannau hyn fe ddaeth cyfle iddi dreulio cyfnod yng nghwmni'r arbenigwr byd-enwog Bernard Berenson yn ei villa crand yn yr Eidal a chael ei chyflwyno i ogoniannau celf cyfnod y Dadeni.

Hanes gwahanol iawn oedd hanes R.S., pan gyfarfu ag Elsi am y tro cyntaf. Ciwrad plwyfol, distadl, cyfyng iawn ei brofiadau a'i orwelion oedd e, er fod awydd arno fe eisoes i ddatblygu'n fardd. Os oedd hi'n *somebody*, yna dim ond *wannabe* naïf iawn oedd R.S. y pryd hynny. Ddegawdau'n ddiweddarach fe wnaeth e gydnabod o bryd i'w gilydd – er yn ddigon amharod – mai Elsi oedd wedi ei osod e ar ben y ffordd i fod yn fardd go iawn, am ei bod hi wedi gwneud iddo fe sylweddoli am y tro cyntaf fod yn rhaid wrth ymroddiad llwyr, di-ildio, cyn medru hawlio bod yn artist cyflawn.

Ac ar un ystyr, roedd y *modus vivendi* priodasol a fabwysiadwyd gan R.S. ac Elsi yn ddrych i'w galwedigaethau gwahanol. Hyd y bo modd, fe gysegrwyd un rhan o'r ficerdy i Elsi, gan gydnabod ei hangen hi fel artist gweledol am olau a gofod. Ac fe neilltuwyd rhyw encilfan arall ar gyfer R.S. a'i farddoni. Prin iawn, yn ôl pob sôn, y bu'r cyfnewid profiad rhyngddyn nhw, ac ar hyd ei hoes fe fynnai Elsi, yn berffaith gywir, na wyddai R.S. ddim oll am luniau. Roedd e'n gwbl anneallus ac anllythrennog i'r cyfeiriad hwnnw. Ond fe wnaeth ei gorau i'w oleuo.

Roedd y ddau ohonyn nhw'n hoff iawn o grwydro'r caeau yn chwilio am ysbrydoliaeth. Ac yn wir, wrth i ryw chwedloniaeth ryfedd Gothig gael ei nyddu o gwmpas R.S., fel yr âi'n fwyfwy enwog a'i drin fel cawr canibalaidd, fe aeth y si ar led ei fod e'n hoff o gasglu penglogau adar ac anifeiliaid mân, a bod y rhain i'w gweld yn tywyllu pob twll a chornel o'r ficerdy. Ond y gwir amdani, oedd mai Elsi'r artist ac nid R.S. oedd yn trysori'r creiriau hyn. Bach iawn o groes-ffrwythloni a gafwyd rhwng celfyddyd Elsi a chelfyddyd R.S. ac er fod cryn dipyn o barch gan y naill at ddawn y llall, amharod iawn oedd R.S. i ganmol Elsi'n gyhoeddus. Yn wir, fe fentrwn i awgrymu'n betrus y gallai fod rhyw gymaint o eiddigedd yn y bardd o ddawn yr artist; ac os felly, yna fe all fod ymdrech anfwriadol i danseilio awdurdod celf weledol ymhlŷg yn y modd y mae R.S. yn trin lluniau yn ei gerddi. Prin iawn y'i ceir yn cydnabod dieithrwch gwaith celf, ac yn parchu ei arwahanrwydd. Mae ysfa ynddo fe bob adeg i gymathu lluniau i'w ddibenion penodol, obsesiynol ef ei hun, ac mae'n barod iawn nid yn unig i ddiystyrru 'ystyr' cynhenid darlun ond hefyd i'w ddatgymalu a'i ddadadeiladu.

Ac eto, roedd gwaith Elsi ac R.S. yn medru cyd-gynganeddu
o bryd i'w gilydd. Yr adeg pan oedd hi wrthi'n gweithio fel un
o dîm o artistiaid rhyfel a gyflogwyd gan y Llywodraeth i greu
cofnod gweledol o adeiladau hynafol y Gymru wledig a oedd
dan fygythiad, roedd R.S. yn cychwyn ar y broses o lunio darlun
testunol cymhleth o Iago Prytherch, gwerinwr gwydn, garw oedd
hefyd yn cynrychioli cyfnod a chymdeithas a fu. Ac roedd ganddo
lygaid llawn mor graff a sylwgar â'i llygaid treiddgar hithau. Ond
wrth i R.S. y bardd ddechrau ennill bri fe giliodd Elsi a'i dawn i'r
cysgodion, yn bennaf am ei bod hi wedi ei aberthu drwy ymroi'n
gyfan gwbl i gynhyrchu gwaith masnachol er mwyn talu am
ddanfon eu mab, Gwydion, i ysgolion bonedd yn Lloegr. Ac fel
y nododd Gwydion ei hun, fe roedd hi hefyd o bryd i'w gilydd
yn ceisio hyfforddi R.S. yn elfennau symlaf hanes celf, drwy
ddyfeisio gêm 'Happy Families' a seiliwyd ar gasglu lluniau o'r un
cyfnod neu gan yr un artist. Talcen digon caled, mae'n bur debyg,
gan ei fod e wedi ei drwytho yn yr hen ragfarn biwritanaidd
yn erbyn lluniau, am eu bod nhw'n arwynebol, yn ddisylwedd,
yn rhy gnawdol ac yn rhy nwydus. Fe gwynodd R.S. mewn un
ysgrif, er enghraifft, nad oedd pwrpas darlunio hen gapel syml
swynol 'Maes-yr-Onnen' am nad oedd modd yn y byd cyfleu'n
weledol wir rin a chyfaredd ysbrydol y fath le. Ac yn wir fe aeth
e cyn belled â chyfeirio'n ddirmygus at hoff gyfrwng ei wraig, sef
dyfrliw, wrth ddamnio ei apel i'r mwyafrif sef yr *hoi polloi*.

I fod yn deg, yr hyn oedd ganddo fe mewn golwg yn yr achos
olaf hwn oedd arfer arlunwyr Saesneg o'r ddeunawfed ganrif hyd
at ganol y ganrif ddiwethaf, o drin Cymru fel dim ond tirwedd
fynyddig ddengar, gan lwyr anwybyddu'r trigolion a'u hiaith a'u
diwylliant. Ac fe'i ceir yn llunio cerdd ymysodol o wrth-fugeiliol
yn achos 'The Welsh Hill Country,' lle mae e'n wfftio hoffder

arlunwyr o beintio defaid wedi eu gosod yn rhamantus gan ganolbwyntio'n heriol o ddadlennol yn lle hynny ar y *fluke*, a'r pry genwair.

Mae'n wir fod ambell gerdd yn trin paentiad yn cael ei chynnwys gan R.S. yn rhai o'i gasgliadau cynnar, ond fe roedd e 'mhell dros ei drigain cyn iddo fe fentro cynnwys cyfres sylweddol o luniau darlun, a hynny yn y gyfrol *Between Here and Now* (1981). Ymateb y mae e i dri deg a thri o luniau gan yr Argraffiadwyr mwyaf enwog, ac mae'n amlwg ddigon yn syth o'r cychwyn ei fod e'n syllu arnyn nhw nid drwy lygaid artist ond drwy lygaid offeiriad sydd megis yn 'fardd-bregethwr' a'i fryd yn bennaf ar foesoli. Yr hyn a ddaw i'r wyneb yn amlwg ddigon hefyd yw rhai o brif obsesiynau personol R.S., am ei fod e'n cael hyd i fynegiant parod grymus o'r rheini yn y delweddau hyn. Dyna chi ei broblemau lu â'r rhyw deg, er enghraifft, problemau yr oedd e'n dueddol iawn i feio ar ei berthynas gynnar ddwys, gymhleth â'i fam. Dro ar ôl tro mae'n lladd ar ystrywiau merched, ar eu rhagrith nhw, ac ar yr ysfa ddifaol sydd ynddyn nhw i rwydo ac i ddifetha dynion. Mae e'n barod iawn i gysylltu cnawdolrwydd merched gyda chnawdolrwydd meddwol a pheryglus paent ar gynfas, gan awgrymu ymhellach fod paent yn nwylo artist yn ymdebygu i 'golur', gan mai'r prif bwrpas yn y naill achos a'r llall yw i dwyllo dynion. Ond mae'n dechrau arbrofi i gyfeiriadau eraill hefyd, gan sylweddoli am y tro cyntaf fod gan luniau allu unigryw i'n gwneud ni'n ymwybodol o'r wedd annaearol (sef 'unheimlich') ar ein bodolaeth meidrol. Fe allan nhw felly fod o wasanaeth ysbrydol hynod werthfawr inni. At hynny y mae e'n cyfeirio pan yn sôn yn awgrymog am 'the brush's piety' ac fe ddychwela droeon yn y ddarlith hon at y sythwelediad allweddol hwnnw.

Yn 1985 cyhoeddwyd *Ingrowing Thoughts*, cyfrol gyfan o gerddi darlun o'i waith. Ynddi mae R.S. yn camu o fyd yr Argraffiadwyr i fyd yr Ôl-Argraffiadwyr a'r Swrrealwyr. A dyma fe felly'n cychwyn ymbellhau oddi wrth y math o luniau yr arbenigai Kyffin Williams ynddynt. Fe osodir cyweirnod y gyfrol wrth i R.S. ymateb i ddarlun ysgytwol o chwyldroadol Picasso, *Guernica*. Fe wêl ynddo ymdrech arwrol artist i lunio celfyddyd gwbl newydd, y gelfyddyd y mae'n rhaid wrthi os am wynebu realiti dreng hunllef y byd modern. Darlun ydyw sydd nid yn unig yn cofnodi dinistr tref ond hefyd chwalfa ddidrugaredd holl etifeddiaeth a thraddodiad celf weledol diwylliant y Gorllewin. Canlyniad dehongliad y dychymyg yma o'r dinistr meddai R.S., yw datgymaliad ffrwydrol yr holl gonfensiynau cyfansoddol hynny a arferai bennu a rheoli celfyddyd. Ac mae R.S. yn holi, pwy fedr ail-adeiladu 'the bones jigsaw?'

Yn y bydysawd newydd arswydus hwn, lle troir pob peth ben i waered, y mae hen drefn gyfarwydd gofod ac amser a arferai'n hangori ni'n gysurus oddi fewn i'n bydasawd wedi ei ddileu yn gyfan gwbl. Fe amlygir hyn yn glir, meddai R.S., yn narlun Ben Shahn, 'Father and Child.' Llun ydyw sy'n dad-wneud y darlun traddodiadol o'r Forwyn Fair a'i Baban. Darlun oedd hwnnw lle y canolbwyntiwyd ar gorff yr un bach yn arffed ei fam am fod y ddelwedd ganolog sanctaidd honno yn hoelio'r byd gweledol cyfan yn ei le, gan osod trefn ddwyfol ar dreigl amser ac ar siâp gofod. Ond nid yw'r fath ffydd yng nghyfeiriad a phwrpas y cosmos yn bosib inni bellach yn sgil darganfyddiadau Darwin a'r gwyddonwyr Ffiseg, nac yn dilyn ffrwydriad y bom atomig. A chan fod yn rhaid i'r artist gwir fodern – boed yn beintiwr neu'n fardd – gydnabod hynny a'i wynebu'n ddewr o onest yn ei gelfyddyd mae'n anorfod fod celfyddyd hefyd yn gorfod cael ei gweddnewid yn llwyr cyn medru cyfateb i'r realiti newydd.

Dyma gyrraedd trobwynt, felly, yn natblygiad R.S. ei hun fel bardd, ac o hyn ymlaen mae gan gelfyddyd weledol ei chyfran yn ei ddatblygiad ysbrydol e hefyd, yn enwedig ar ôl iddo fe gefnu i bob pwrpas ar yr Eglwys yng Nghymru drwy benderfynu ymddeol yn gynnar fel offeiriad. Doedd hi ddim yn syndod llwyr i fi, felly, pan y des i ar draws gasgliad o luniau darlun ymhlith y llawysgrifau hynny a adawyd ar ei ôl. Bellach mae Tony Brown a Jason Walford Davies wedi golygu detholiad o'r cerddi hyn a'u cyhoeddi yn y gyfrol hardd, drawiadol *Too Brave to Dream: Encounters with Modern Art* a gyhoeddwyd yn ddiweddar gan Bloodaxe. Felly, fe hoffwn i ganolbwyntio ar rai o'r prif themâu y mae'r farddoniaeth yn eu trin.

Rwy'n cychwyn gyda Jankel Adler a'i ddarlun o Dafydd, y bugail ifanc yn yr Hen Destament a orchmynwyd i chwarae ei delyn hudolus o swynol wrth erchwyn gwely'r Brenin Saul mewn ymdrech i gael gwared ar ei hunllefau. Iddew o wlad Pwyl oedd Adler a gollodd naw aelod o'i deulu yn yr Holocost. Ac er na wyddai R.S. am hynny, mae'n trin y darlun fel cyfaddefiad yr artist modern, boed e'n arlunydd neu'n fardd, o'i ddiymadferthedd dirdynnol a'r anallu byddai yn ei lorio pan y disgwylir iddo fe arfer ei ddawn i fynegi erchyllterau eithaf y byd modern. Oherwydd, nid tannau y mae'r Dafydd hwn yn ceisio cyffwrdd â nhw, ond rhes filain o weirennau pigog yr un fath â ddefnyddiwyd i amlgylchynu uffern Auschwitz, felly mae'r arlunydd wedi ei ddelweddu'n ceisio ymgodymu â thelyn oedd yn ei drechu. Ac awgrymir yn gryf fod yr un ysbryd drwg a aflonyddai ar y Brenin Saul hefyd yma megis yn gwawdio ymdrechion ofer yr 'artist' Dafydd i'w ddofi. Ar un olwg, y mae'r gerdd yn fy atgoffa i o gyfaddefiadau arswydus cyson R.S. yn rhai o gerddi ei gyfnod olaf ei fod e'n dal i gael ei erlid gan y 'Furies'. *No Truce with the Furies* oedd teitl ei gasgliad olaf un, ac fe gofiwch chi mai'r Furies, yn ôl yr hen chwedl Roegaidd, wnaeth boenydio ac erlid y cerddor Orffeus, gan orffen drwy ei ddarnio fe'n fyw fesul pob aelod o'i gorff.

Fydde fe ddim yn gwbl amhriodol, yn fy marn i, inni drin y darlun hwn gan Adler a'r gerdd gyfatebol fel rhyw fath o flaen-ddarlun ac epigraff ar gyfer y gyfrol *Too Brave to Dream* ar ei hyd. Oherwydd ymgais gan R.S. yw'r gyfrol gyfan i lunio cerddi sy'n mentro wynebu heriau byd echrydus. Cyffyrddir â'r un testun yn y gerdd am lun gan Henry Moore o berson yn cysgu er diogelwch ar blatform yr Underground yn Llundain adeg yr Ail Ryfel Byd. Fe fydd dihuno, medde R.S., yn golygu dod wyneb yn wyneb â gweddillion y trueiniaid hynny a laddwyd gan y bomiau; y rhai hynny a oedd 'too brave to dream.'

'Too brave to dream,' sef yn rhy ddewr i gilio o fyd y bom i fyd breuddwyd, neu, yn achos R.S. ei hun: rhy ddewr i gilio o olwg y byd cyfoes a llochesu mewn barddoniaeth gysurus gonfensiynol. Ac o syllu'n fanylach ar y testun, fe sylwch ar sawl enghraifft bwysig o arfer R.S. o orffen llinell cyn fod ystyr y cymal neu'r frawddeg yn glir, gan demtio'r darllenydd i gamgymryd gweddill y datganiad.

Nid dyfais rethregol glyfar yw hon yn unig. Yn hytrach mae'n fodd i'r testun ddeffro ynom ymwybyddiaeth fod ein hymateb ni nid yn unig i eiriau ond hefyd i fyd profiad ei hun yn ymateb ystrydebol, a'n bod ni'n gaeth i hen arferion. Anodd iawn yw hi i ni'r darllenwyr, yr un modd ag yw hi i'r bardd, ddeffro o'n trwmgwsg cyfforddus a wynebu realiti pethau. Dywedai T.S Eliot nad oedd dynoliaeth yn medru dygymod â gormod o realiti.

Mae'r farddoniaeth yn ein herio ninnau, hefyd, i fentro bod yn rhy ddewr i ddianc i barth breuddwydion.

Ac os sylweddolwn ni hynny, yna fe ddeallwn ni, hefyd, paham fod R.S. wedi dewis symud oddi wrth ei ddiddordeb cynnar yn yr artistiaid Argraffiadol ac wedi ffoli fwyfwy yn ei henaint ar gynnyrch yr Ôl-argraffiadwyr a'r Swrrealwyr. Oherwydd dyma'r gelfyddyd wirioneddol chwyldroadol, yn ei brofiad ef, a fedrai ddelweddu gwallgofrwydd y byd dynol bellach, ac a fedrai agor cil drws y meddwl ar ddirgelion y tu hwnt i gyrraedd y rheswm – dirgelion yr ystyriai yn ddirgelion ysbrydol yn y bôn. Er mwyn goleuo'r pwynt hwn, fe wna'i droi nesaf at ddarlun Yves Tanguy, *Terre d'Ombre*, sef Gwlad y Cysgodion. Ynddo, debygwn i roedd R.S. yn gweld awgrym o Dir Neb, rhostir diffaith y Rhyfel Mawr, neu grindir ôl-niwclear.

Anialdir: Diwedd y Byd: Dydd y Farn: dyna ddehongliad R.S. o'r darlun hwn. Y mae darlun Tanguy yn cywasgu dau o ofnau dyfnaf, mwyaf arswydus R.S., sef ofn bygythion enbyd y byd niwclear a'r pryder fod ymwrthod dyn â Duw, a dewis y dyn modern i addoli grym y rheswm a'i gynhyrchion, yn paratoi'r ffordd yn anorfod ar gyfer trychineb catastroffaidd. A'r ddelwedd ddieflig a fathwyd gan R.S. i grynhoi'r ail arswyd hwn yw 'The Machine.' 'The Machine' yw'r anghenfil sy'n brif elyn R.S. y bardd. Hwn sy'n dileu'n hymwybyddiaeth achubol ni o fod yn eneidiau unigryw, prin. A dyna pam mai R.S. yn proffwydo y daw dydd pan fydd Duw yn methu'n hatgyfodi ni o farw i fyw am na fydd modd iddo fe bellach ein hadnabod ni wrth ein henw. Fe ddilewyd ein hunaniaeth yn llwyr. Fe welir Duw'n crwydro'r tir diffaith, 'Wandering' gair sy'n cael ei gysgodi yma, megis, gan y gair hiraethlon 'wondering.'

Ac o ddilyn y trywydd hwn ychydig ymhellach, fe sylweddolwn

ni mai un o briod ddyletswyddau y bardd modern, ym marn R.S., oedd gwarchod geiriau a diogelu enwau, gan fod dynoldeb y ddynoliaeth yn annatod glwm â hygrededd gair. Dyma'r thema rwyf am ei ddilyn nesaf. Er mwyn paratoi'r ffordd at ystyried barn R.S. am swyddogaeth yr artist yn y broses o barchu rhyfeddod prin yr unigolyn, rwy'n benthyg ymadrodd trawiadol a fathwyd ganddo fe am 'coloured excrement' o balet yr artist. Darlun gan André Derain sydd gan R.S. mewn golwg, â'r teitl 'hunan-bortread yr artist.'

Fel sy'n wybyddus i nifer ohonoch chi, rwy'n siwr, fe gyfaddefodd R.S. droeon nad oedd e erioed wedi medru amgyffred ei hun. Roedd ei fodolaeth unigryw ef yn dal yn ddirgelwch dryslyd iddo fe hyd y diwedd. Ac fe ddatblygodd e ddau esboniad gwahanol ar darddiad yr ansicrwydd mewnol dirfodol hanfodol hwnnw. Esboniad seicolegol oedd y naill – sef fod ei berthynas afiach â'i fam wedi ei atal yn ifanc rhag datblygu sicrwydd annibynnol gwaelodol. Ond esboniad metaffisigol ac ysbrydol oedd y llall; sef mai mynegiant o'i ymwybyddiaeth briodol e o ddiddymrwydd bodolaeth pob unigolyn meidrol pitw yng nghyd-destun dirgelion annirnad y cread, oedd yr ymdeimlad eneidiol o fod yn 'neb.' Ac fe wnaeth R.S. archwilio'r ddwy wedd hon ar ei ddiffyg hunaniaeth mewn dwy gyfrol arbennig o feistrolgar, sef ei hunangofiant rhyfedd *Neb* ac *The Echoes Return Slow,* plethwaith cywrain, cymhleth o ryddiaith ac o farddoniaeth.

A dyma chi'r cyd-destun sydd, yn fy marn i, yn goleuo ystyr ei gerdd e am ddarlun André Derain. Yn ôl R.S. erfynodd yr artist ar ei 'dry brush' i'w enwi. Ar y darlleniad cyntaf, fe gymerwn ni'n ganiataol mai gorchymyn awdurdodol plaen yw'r geiriau hyn; gorchymyn yr artist i'w gyfrwng amlygu hanfod ei hunaniaeth yn glir drwy ei alw wrth ei enw priod. Ond yr eildro y darllennwn

ni'r geiriau fe ddaw ystyr arall i'r wyneb, a hwnnw'n fynegiant nid
o hyder ond o betrusrwydd. Oherwydd nid gorchymyn yn unig
mo hynny y tro hwn, ond hefyd deisyfiad ingol. Dyma'r artist yn
ymbil ar ei gyfrwng (sef paent) i ddatgelu iddo fe'r hyn na ŵyr:
sef pwy yn union ydyw. Ymbil y mae am hunan-ddatguddiad
sy'n hunan-ddarganfyddiad, yn hytrach na gorchymyn hunan-
fynegiant. Mae'r artist bellach yn sylweddoli fod y weithred o
beintio'r darlun yn fodd unigryw, cwbl anhepgorol iddo fe ddod
wyneb yn wyneb â hanfod eneidiol ei fod ei hun. Mae'r weithred
o beintio felly yn weithred seicolegol ac eneidiol datguddiol.
Rhyfeddod pellach yw mai dim ond drwy ymhel â chyfrwng
synhwyrus mor fras, mor ffiaidd o gyntefig ar un olwg, â phaent y
gall yr artist brofi'r wyrth hon. Ac wrth gwrs, nid artist gweledol
oedd gan R.S. mewn golwg yn unig. Fe roedd e hefyd yn synied
am artist geiriau. Wedi'r cyfan, onid ei arwr mawr e, W. B. Yeats,
a fynnai fod y farddoniaeth fwyaf aruchel a throsgynnol yn codi
o laid a llaca'n gwythiennau ni? Dim ond drwy chwarae â geiriau,
fel bydd plentyn bach yn ddigon parod i chwarae â'i faw ei hun, y
mae bardd yn medru darganfod pwy yn wir ydyw.

Ac y mae R.S. yn cyffwrdd â'r un testun mewn cerdd arall
sy'n ymateb i ddarlun Gabriel Robin, *Yr Aelwyd*. Yn y gerdd
ymatebol hon y mae R.S. unwaith yn rhagor yn ystyried lluniau a
cherddi fel ei gilydd yn fydwragedd ein hymdrechion ni i ddwyn
y gwirioneddau gwaelodol amdanom ni'n hunain i'r golau.
Unwaith yn rhagor dyma arlunydd yn chwilio am ei hunaniaeth
ddirgel ef ei hun, drwy chwilio am olion wyneb yn y marwydos.
Ond ofer yw ei ymdrech, gan mai dim ond 'anonymity' sydd i'w
weld yn y mudlosgi o'i flaen. Pwysleisir unwaith yn rhagor yn
y darlun hwn nad dull o fynegi'r hunan yw llun na cherdd ond
cyfrwng sydd o werth unigryw inni. Mae hyn am ei fod ef yn

ein galluogi ni i chwilio am – a weithiau hyd yn oed i gael cip annisgwyl ar – ein hunaniaeth eneidiol.

Sylwch am eiliad ar y defnydd o'r gair bach cyfarwydd diniwed yna 'discover,' pan yw R.S. yn sôn am ddarganfod wyneb yn y cols sy'n syllu ar yr arlunydd ei hun. Oherwydd y mae e gyfystyr nid yn unig â 'realise,' ond hefyd 'uncover.' Dad-lennu cuddfan eithaf yr hunan: dyna'r grym anhepgor y mae llun a cherdd fel ei gilydd yn meddu arno fe. Cerdd yw hon am gyfatebion cymesur – y mae'r marwydos yn ddrych i'r enaid, ac y mae'r enaid yn ddrych i'r marwydos. A sylwch shwd mae R.S. yn llunio cerdd sydd hithe'n awgrymu cymesuredd. Er enghraifft, mae'n gosod y gair allweddol 'warmth' yn yr union un man ar ddechrau dwy linell yn olynol. Ond os taw am bwysleisio brastod cyfrwng yr artist a'r bardd oedd R.S. yn y gerdd am lun Derain, yr hyn y mae e am ei bwysleisio'r tro hwn yw hynawsedd cynnes y cyfrwng, a'i barodrwydd i wasanaethu gofynion yr hunan.

Thema amlwg arall yn *Too Brave to Dream*, mae R.S. yn ei grynhoi mewn ymadrodd ergydiol o fachog yw'r "Contraceptive of art". Fe ddaw'r ddelwedd annisgwyl hon o gerdd yn ymateb i ddarn gan Man Ray â'r teitl moel 'gwrthrych.' Gadewch i fi grynhoi'n fyr ddiddordeb R.S. yn y darn hynod hwn o waith, cyn troi at y gerdd ei hun. Yr hyn sy'n ei gyfareddu fe yw'r modd y mae'r gwrthrych rhyfedd dieithr hwn o waith Man Ray rywsut yn ystyrlon i ni, er nad yw e'n cyfateb i unrhyw wrthrych hysbys. Ac i R.S. mae hynny'n awgrymu'n bod ni'n medru synhwyro dirgelwch eithaf ein bodolaeth a'n bydysawd, er ei fod e'n llwyr y tu hwnt i amgyffred ein deall ni. Trwy ddehongli'r darn yn y modd hwn mae R.S. yn ein hatgoffa ni fod 'na sawl ffrwd bwysig yn cyfrannu at ddatblygiad celfyddyd Fodernaidd ar ddechrau'r ugeinfed ganrif. Dyna chi anthropoleg, er enghraifft, a'r diddordeb yng nghynnyrch llwythau 'cyntefig.' Ac wrth gwrs, fe feddyliwn ni'n syth hefyd am seicdreiddiad ac am ddarganfyddiadau Freud a'i gyfoeswyr o'r isymwybod a dyfnderoedd anghaffael y meddwl dynol. Ond roedd yno hefyd ffrwd a ddeilliai o theosoffiaethau o gredoau anuniongred eraill tebyg ac fe amlygir y wedd hon ar Foderniaeth droeon dros gyfnod hir o amser sy'n ymestyn o gyfnod Kandinsky, a'i draethawd yn trin y wedd ysbrydol ar gelfyddyd hyd at luniau unlliw hwyr Mark Rothko.

Ond beth felly yw ystyr yr ymadrodd 'the contraceptive of art'?

Mae darlun neu gerdd yn caniatáu inni gyfathrach fynwesol barod ag ef ond mae hefyd yn ein hatal ni rhag ei berchnogi'n llawn. Nid oes modd inni aralleirio ystyr cerdd, gan ei thrin hi fel petai'n ddim ond datganiad o'r cyfarwydd. Yn ei hanfod, mae ystyr ac arwyddocâd cerdd yn ddihysbydd o annirnad, yr un fath ag ystyr ac arwyddocâd gwrthrych Man Ray. Ac felly mae'n cynnig delwedd inni o fodolaeth annirnad pob bod byw. Mae'r hyn a ddywedodd Hugh McDiarmid am y cread yn wir hefyd am gelfyddyd o bob math: 'its prodigiousness is a safeguarding excellence.' 'Prodigiousness' am ei fod e'n gorlifo'n hamgyffred ni. Ond pam 'safeguarding excellence'? Oherwydd bod celfyddyd yn gwarchod ei ddirgelwch ei hunan y mae hefyd yn ein hachub ni rhag y duedd haerllug sydd ynom i gredu'n bod ni'n medru mesur union hyd a lled pob person byw a phob peth sy'n bod. Ac mae mawr angen ein harbed arnom ni, ym marn R.S., am fod yr ysfa ddifaol hyn i esbonio yn rhemp yn y byd modern, gan fod llwyddiannau ysgubol technoleg yn rhoi rhydd heol iddo fe. Ac i R.S., dyma wir Gwymp y ddynoliaeth; y broses o ddad-ddynoli.

Oherwydd hyn, y mae R.S. yn arfer trin darlun neu gerflun fel petai'n bôs, hynny yw yn 'riddle' na ellir ei ddatrys. Mae'n

werth nodi wrth fynd heibio fod y gair 'enigma' yn deillio mae'n
debyg o'r gair Groeg am 'bôs.' Ac mae R.S. yn creu cerddi sy'n
dwyllodrus o syml, gan fwriadu eu bod nhw yn amwys eu hystyr
dan yr wyneb. Fe ellir cyffelybu'r cerddi diweddar hyn i'r posau
a'r paradocsau hynny y mae mynach Zen yn eu parchu ac a elwir
yn koans. Y diffyniad a geir o koan mewn geiriadur Saesneg yw 'a
paradox to be meditated upon that is used by Zen Buddhist monks
to abandon ultimate dependence on reason and to force them into
gaining sudden enlightenment.' Un enghraifft o hynny sy'n hen
gyfarwydd i ni yn y Gorllewin yw'r cwestiwn bachog 'What is the
sound of one hand clapping?' Un arall yw 'What is your original
face before your father and mother were born.' Ac yn arwyddocaol
ddigon, ac ystyried mai bardd yw R.S., mae'n debyg fod y koan
wedi deillio o gemau geiriol, megis gosod teitl ymddangosiadol
anaddas ar gerdd, neu'r arfer o amwyso geiriau'n gelfydd.

Ac fe welir R.S. yn myfyrio uwchben pynciau fel hyn yn y
gerdd lle mae'n ymateb i ddarlun Matta, 'Le vertige d'Eros.' Yr
hyn y mae R.S. am ei bwysleisio yn y gerdd yw mai paradocs yw
hanfod y darlun, gan ei fod, yr un fath â gwrthrych Man Ray,
yn enghraifft o gyfansoddiad di-ystyr ystyrlon. Ac felly mae'n
nodweddu hanfod pob gwaith celf yn ddiwahân. Mae darlun o'r
fath hwn o werth arbennig i fardd, gan fod disgwyl cyfeiliornus
i brydydd arfer geiriau er mwyn datgan rhyw neges ystyrlon.
Yr unig ymateb priodol i'r disgwyliad hwn, ym marn R.S., yw'r
datganiad moel 'pe bawn i'n gwybod beth mae'r gerdd yn ei
ddweud fyddwn i ddim wedi trafferthu i lunio'r gerdd yn y lle
cyntaf; yn hytrach fe fyddwn i wedi datgan fy neges yn blaen.'

Yn y gerdd sy'n cyfateb i'r ddelwedd, fe welwch chi fod R.S.
yn gwneud sbri am ben yr ieithwedd a ddatblygwyd ganddom ni
i ddisgrifio a thrwy hynny ddisgrifio llun – 'line, composition,

tonal value' ac ati. Oherwydd, yn y bôn 'does gan y rhain ddim oll i'w ddatgelu am wir ystyr unrhyw gyfansoddiad. Ac fe sylwch chi ar yr wrtheb slei a geir ar ddiwedd y gerdd, lle mae R.S. yn sôn am y paentiad bron yn mynnu mewn modd *'almost* inaudible': ond os posib fod llun yn medru yngan sŵn? Wel na, mae'n amlwg ddim. Beth, felly, sydd gan R.S. mewn golwg? Wel, fe dybiwn i ei fod e am awgrymu fod llun yn gwneud ei orau glas i 'ddweud' wrthon ni mai llun yn unig yw, ac nid datganiad, ond ein bod ni'n styfnig o glust-fyddar i'w neges. Ac y mae'r un peth yn wir am gerdd, er mai o eiriau y'i gwnaed hi yn hytrach na phaent. Ry'n ni mor drwm ein clyw fel mai prin bellach y medrwn ni glywed sibrwd islais pob cerdd mai nid datganiad ydyw. Ac fe ellir mynd cam ymhellach, gan fod R.S. yn argyhoeddedig fod yr un yn wir am y ddynoliaeth. Ry'n ni'n rhy fyddar mwyach i fedru clywed yr enaid yn sibrwd wrthym yn daer nad oes modd cael ato, nac inni afael yn ein hanfod ni'n hunain, drwy arfer y rheswm. Fel yr awgryma R.S. mewn man arall, yn sgil y chwyldro a grewyd gan wyddoniaeth a thechnoleg, nodwedd y bywyd modern yw ei fod e'n 'glib with prose.' Ry'n ni felly yn trin cerdd fel petai'n ddarn o ryddiaith gyffredin.

Darlun arall sy'n arwain R.S. i'r un casgliad yw llun Salvador Dali 'Y Wawr' (Phantasmagoria). Y sylw mwyaf deallus am y darlun ac am y gerdd gyfatebol yw'r sylw craff a wnaed gan René Magritte pan y gofynnwyd iddo fe esbonio ei waith. Beth yw lluniau, medde fe, ond delweddau gweledol sy'n cuddio dim. Dro arall, fe wnaeth Magritte sylw sy'n hynod berthnasol i ddull R.S. o ddehongli lluniau *Too Brave to Dream*. 'Mae'r uniad o bethau sy'n ymddangos yn ddi-berthynas i'w gilydd yn fy ngwaith ' meddai Magritte, 'yn awgrymu dirgelwch hanfodol y byd'. Ac ar un ystyr, y mae'r dirgelwch i'w weld yn glir ar wyneb llun, ac ar wyneb ein bywyd, pe bai ganddon ni'r llygaid i'w gweld. Ac yn ei ymdrech i ddatgelu'r gwirionedd gwaelodol hwnnw, sydd eto'n wirionedd plaen, mae R.S. dro ar ôl tro yn llwyr anwybyddu yr hyn sydd gan artist a'i ddarlun mewn golwg. Chewch chi ddim gwell enghraifft o'i ddull croes-graen e o ddehongli llun na'i ymateb i ddarlun Edvard Munch, 'Y Tŷ Dan y Coed.' Mae'r teitl, yr un fath â chyfansoddiad y darlun ei hun, yn cyfeirio'n sylw ni'n berffaith glir a diamwys at y tŷ mawr sy wedi ei osod yn go agos at ganol y darlun. Ond mae'n arfer greddfol gan R.S. ddehongli darlun wyneb i waered, gan bwysleisio'r cefndir yn hytrach na'r blaendir, a gan gychwyn drwy graffu ar gorneli ac ymylon y cyfansoddiad. Felly, mae'n mynnu syllu, yn ei gerdd, nid ar y tŷ ond ar y grŵp o bobl sy'n llechu ar y dde yng nghornel gwaelod y darlun. Ac ar ben hynny, mae'n mynnu fod y rhain yn cuddio o dan y ddaear, er ei bod hi'n amlwg ddigon eu bod nhw'n sefyll yn normal ac yn gadarn ar wyneb y tir. Pen draw hyn oll yw fod R.S. yn medru awgrymu mai rhyw fath o grŵp o wrthryfelwyr cudd yw'r grŵp hwn o bobl, tebyg i'r 'Underground' adeg y rhyfel ond mai cuddio y mae'r rhain nid o olwg y Gestapo ond o afael 'the Gestapo of time.' Dyma ichi enghraifft ardderchog, felly, o'r modd y bydd R.S. yn ddi-ffael yn chwilio am gyfle i ddehongli darlun yn ôl ei fympwyon a'i obsesiynau ef ei hun. Oherwydd yr hyn mae'n ei weld yn narlun Munch yw arwydd o'r un penderfyniad sydd i'w weld ym marddoniaeth R.S. ei hun, sef penderfynad i chwalu gafael haearnaidd byd amser ar ein meddyliau, er mwyn ein gwneud ni'n ymwybodol mai bodau eneidiol, ac felly brodorion y tragwyddol, yr ydyn ni yn ein hanfod.

A dyma fi bron wedi dod i ddiwedd fy nhrafodaeth. Ond fedra i ddim rhoi to ar y mwdwl tan i fi ddwyn eich sylw chi at y gerdd orau oll yn y casgliad *Too Brave to Dream*, cerdd sy hefyd ymhlith y cerddi crefyddol gorau a sgrifennwyd gan R.S. yn fy marn i. Ymateb y mae'r gerdd i lun cyfareddol o ryfedd yr artist swrrealaidd o wlad Czech, Toyen, llun â'r teitl *Hlas Vesa* (Llais y Goedwig). Ac mae'n amlwg ddigon ei bod hi'n ymweud â diddordeb ysol R.S. yn nirgelwch y Duwdod annirnad, cudd. Ymateb y mae i ddelwedd sy'n ymdebygu'n fras i dylluan. Ond o graffu, fe wêl nad oes ganddi na chrafangau na phig nac hyd yn oed llygaid. Felly, ni ŵyr R.S. sut yn union i'w henwi. Mae'n ymwybodol o'r temtasiwn i'w hanwybyddu, am nad yw'n wrthrych y gall y rheswm ei ddirnad o gwbl; ond mae'r ddelwedd hynod hon yn cyniwair ei ddychymyg fel na all wneud hynny, ac mae'n cydnabod fod yna ryw adlais yn codi o eigion ei enaid yn mynnu ei fod yn cydnabod delwedd sy'n edrych arnom heb lygaid a heb geg sy'n llefaru.

'Ei luniad yn oleuni': ymdrech gan Euros Bowen yw'r ymadrodd cofiadwy hwn i ddathlu y grym llachar sy gan ddarlun i oleuo'n byd ni. A'r un yn y bôn yw testun moliant R.S. yn ei gerddi darlun ef. Felly, fe fedrir dweud amdano yntau, hefyd, fel bardd a gynhyrchodd gynifer o luniau darlun hynod a nodedig, fod 'ei luniad yn oleuni.' Oherwydd er nad oedd ei ddulliau ystyfnig o wrthnysig e o foli lluniau wrth fodd artist go iawn fel Elsi o gwbl, ac er na fyddai ei syniadau ef yn ei henoed am gelfyddyd weledol yn debyg o daro deuddeg yng nghlyw Kyffin Williams mae'n siwr, fe ddylen ni i gyd fod yn ddiolchgar iawn serch hynny fod R.S. wedi goleuo celfyddyd lluniau inni yn ei ffordd chwithig unigryw ef ei hun.

Precis: 'Ei luniad yn oleuni': R.S. Thomas ym myd lluniau

This essay focuses primarily on R. S. Thomas's responses to paintings in his posthumously published poetry collection *Too Brave to Dream*. Beginning by noting that Thomas was taught how to 'read' pictures by his wife Elsi (Mildred Eldridge) and that his earliest responses to visual art may mostly be found in *Between Here and Now* (the Impressionists) and *Ingrowing Thoughts* (the post-Impressionists and Surrealists), the discussion concludes by examining a series of images from *Too Brave to Dream*. It is suggested that in these ekphrastic poems Thomas explores key issues such as the challenge to find a style of artistic representation adequate to the registering of the many human atrocities of the modern era; a secular age's catastrophic loss of belief in the spiritual dimensions of individual existence, and its resulting obsession with dominance and power; art's responsibility to act as a corrective to this damaging world view; its power to thwart the reductive influence of the hubristic human reason; and its unique ability to access and empower the deep, instinctive healing powers of the psyche. The painting-poems are thus seen as not marginal but integral to the late Thomas's great attempts to produce modern religious poetry.

Yn gyn-Is-Lywydd Cymdeithas Ddysgedig Cymru ac yn Gymrawd yr Academi Brydeinig mae **M. Wynn Thomas** yn Athro'r Saesneg ac yn ddeilydd Cadair Emyr Humphreys yn Llên Saesneg Cymru ym Mhrifysgol Abertawe. Sefydlwyd Canolfan ganddo yn ogystal (CREW) i ymchwilio i'r llên honno. Bu'n Athro ar Ymweliad â Phrifysgol Harvard, a chyhoeddodd dau ddwsin o gyfrolau am farddoniaeth y Taleithiau ac am ddau ddiwylliant llenyddol Cymru. Y diweddaraf o'r rhain yw *The Nations of Wales*, 1890-1915 (2016), *All That is Wales* (2017) a *Cyfan-dir Cymru* (2017). Yn sgil cael ei wneud yn gyfrifol gan R. S. Thomas am y cerddi hynny na chyhoeddwyd ganddo yn ystod ei fywyd, fe olygydd ddetholiad ohonynt â'r teitl *Residues* ym 2002. Ac i nodi canmlwyddiant R. S. Thomas, fe gyhoeddodd astudiaeth o waith y bardd yn 2013 â'r teitl *Serial Obsessive* a gyrhaeddodd restr fer Llyfr y Flwyddyn.

Hawlfraint y Lluniau a Chydnabyddiaeth Ffynonellau
Picture and Copyright Acknowledgements

8. Norma Lopez
   ⓛ *Llyfrgell Genedlaethol Cymru*
   © The National Library of Wales

9. Brychan Evans
   ⓛ *Llyfrgell Genedlaethol Cymru*
   © The National Library of Wales

10. *Euros Hughes yn dyfrhau ei gaeau* / Euros Hughes irrigating his fields
    ⓛ *Llyfrgell Genedlaethol Cymru*
    © The National Library of Wales

11. *Gwartheg duon Cymreig* / Welsh Blacks
    © Gwasg Gregynog

12. *Ffermwyr dan y grib* / Farmers below the ridge
    ⓛ *Ymddiriedolaeth Syr Kyffin Williams*
    © Sir Kyffin Williams Trust

13. *Storm Trearddur* / Storm at Trearddur © Oriel Ynys Môn

14. *Ffermwr a gwartheg* / Farmer and Cattle.
    ⓛ © Oriel Ynys Môn

15. *Moelwyn Bach* © Oriel Ynys Môn

16. *Kyffin yn Nant Peris* / Kyffin at Nant Peris
    © ITV Cymru / Wales

Diolch yn fawr i Lyfrgell Genedlaethol Cymru a'r Ganolfan Uwchefrydiau Cymreig a Cheltaidd am gael defnyddio bywgraffiad Kyffin Williams, rhan o Y Bywgraffiadur Cymreig.

Mae gan y Llyfrgell Brydeinig gyfweliad sain saith awr o hyd gyda Kyffin Williams a recordiwyd gan Cathy Courtney ar gyfer prosiect Artists' Lives. *Symbylwyd* Artists' Lives *yn 1990 gan* National Life

Stories, *ymddiriedolaeth elusennol wedi'i lleoli yn adran hanes llafar Y Llyfrgell Brydeinig, mewn partneriaeth ag Archif y Tate, ac sy'n gweithio yn agos gyda'r Henry Moore Institute. Ei nod yw galluogi artistiaid Prydain i gofnodi eu profiadau yn eu geiriau eu hunain, er mwyn atodi, ehangu neu herio sylwadau gan eraill. Erbyn diwedd 2017 roedd 391 o gyfweliadau hanesion hir oes yn y casgliad. Mae llawer ohonynt gan gynnwys un Kyffin Williams ar gael i wrando arnynt, am ddim ac ar lein drwy wefan Y Llyfrgell Brydeinig. Am rhagor o wybodaeth ewch i* www.bl.uk/nls/artists.

Many thanks to the National Library of Wales and the Centre for Advanced Welsh and Celtic Studies for use of the biography of Kyffin Williams, a part of Y Bywgraffiadur Cymreig.

The British Library holds a seven hour audio interview with Kyffin Williams recorded by Cathy Courtney for the *Artists' Lives* Project. *Artists' Lives* was initiated in 1990 by National Life Stories, the charitable trust based in the oral history section of the British Library, in partnership with Tate Archive and is run in close collaboration with the Henry Moore Institute. Its aim is to enable British artists to create a record of their experiences in their own words to complement, enlarge and sometimes challenge accounts by other commentators. By the end of 2017 there were 391 long life story interviews in the collection and many, including the recording with Kyffin Williams, can be accessed online free of charge via the British Library website. For more information see www.bl.uk/nls/artists. https://sounds.bl.uk/Arts-literature-and-performance/Art/021M-C0466X0024XX-0100V0

Clawr Cefn - Portread o Kyffin gan Bernard Dunstan R.A.
Back Cover – A Portrait of Kyffin by Bernard Dunstan R.A.

KYFFIN
DAN SYLW • IN VIEW